CACHE LEVEL

1

Caring for Children

SECOND EDITION

Corinne Barker
Emma Ward

cache
Endorsed

HODDER
EDUCATION
AN HACHETTE UK COMPANY

Upon successful completion of this qualification, learners will be awarded the NCFE CACHE Level 1 Diploma in Caring for Children 501/1015/9. This CACHE branded qualification is certified by the Awarding Organisation, NCFE.

Every effort has been made to trace all copyright holders, but if any have been inadvertently overlooked, the Publishers will be pleased to make the necessary arrangements at the first opportunity.

Although every effort has been made to ensure that website addresses are correct at time of going to press, Hodder Education cannot be held responsible for the content of any website mentioned in this book. It is sometimes possible to find a relocated web page by typing in the address of the home page for a website in the URL window of your browser.

Hachette UK's policy is to use papers that are natural, renewable and recyclable products and made from wood grown in well-managed forests and other controlled sources. The logging and manufacturing processes are expected to conform to the environmental regulations of the country of origin.

Orders: please contact Bookpoint Ltd, 130 Park Drive, Milton Park, Abingdon, Oxon OX14 4SE. Telephone: +44 (0)1235 827827. Fax: +44 (0)1235 400401. Email education@bookpoint.co.uk Lines are open from 9 a.m. to 5 p.m., Monday to Saturday, with a 24-hour message answering service. You can also order through our website: www.hoddereducation.co.uk

ISBN: 978 1 5104 8560 0

© Corrine Barker and Emma Ward 2020

First published in 2020 by
Hodder Education,
An Hachette UK Company
Carmelite House
50 Victoria Embankment
London EC4Y 0DZ

www.hoddereducation.co.uk

Impression number 10 9 8 7 6 5 4 3 2 1

Year   2024 2023 2022 2021 2020

Cover photo © Samuel B. - stock.adobe.com

Illustrations by Integra Software Services Pvt. Ltd, Pondicherry, India

Typeset by Integra Software Services Pvt. Ltd, Pondicherry, India

Printed in Dubai

A catalogue record for this title is available from the British Library.

Contents

Acknowledgements

Thank you to my colleagues at Wakefield College for all their support and to all the students I have had the pleasure of teaching – you are the ones that inspire me. *Corinne Barker*

To the wonderful Jake, Ben and Eva-May, for your on-going inspiration and support – thank you so much. Thanks also to all the students I have known and taught over the years. You have all been close to mind as I have debated over the words on the page. *Emma Ward*

Dedicated to Grandad Derek and Maz

Photo credits

The Publishers would like to thank the following for permission to reproduce copyright material.

ABC & 123 blocks © iofoto/Fotolia.com, except page 2 & page 56 © Edyta Pawlowska - stock.adobe.com

Page 3 © Grafvision/stock.adobe.com; page 4 © JulesSelmes2014; page 6 © sparkia/stock.adobe.com; page 9 © Beboy/Fotolia.com; page 10 © Luxian/Fotolia.com; page 18 © JulesSelmes2014; page 24 © NiDerLander/Fotolia.com; page 27 © Monkey Business/stock.adobe.com; page 30 © Shutterstock/Ostap Davydiak; page 32 © Pixel-Shot/stock.adobe.com; page 34 © yamasan/stock.adobe.com; page 38 © pololia/stock.adobe.com; page 39 Courtesy William Younger; page 40 © PhotosIndia.com LLC/Alamy Stock Photo; page 42 © Fuse via Getty Images; page 43 © Rayman/Digital Vision/Getty Images; page 45 © Konstantin Yuganov/Fotolia.com; page 49 © sopradit/stock.adobe.com; page 54 © Alexander Raths/Fotolia.com; page 57 © JulesSelmes2014; page 58 © pogonici/stock.adobe.com; page 62 (tr) © picsfive/Fotolia.com, Lion mark © BTHA, CE mark © European Commission via conformance.co.uk; page 63 Courtesy Sue Gascoyne, Play to Z; page 64 © nyulv; page 66 (b) © Beboy/Fotolia.com; page 68 © Irina Fischer/stock.adobe.com; page 70 © JulesSelmes2014; page 71 © JulesSelmes2014; page 75 © Tim Clayton/Corbis via Getty Images; page 77 © Wavebreak Media Ltd/123RF.com; page 81 (t) © JulesSelmes2014, (b) © nyul/Fotolia.com; page 83 Courtesy Bede Academy, Blyth, Northumberland; page 87 © dinostock/Fotolia.com; page 88 (tl) © Tsvetina/stock.adobe.com, (bl) © Tsvetina/stock.adobe.com, (r) © Robert Byron/Fotolia.com; page 92 © Andrey Kiselev/Fotolia.com; page 95 © olesea vetrila/Shutterstock.com; page 96 © Razvan Nitoi/Alamy Stock Photo; page 105 © micromonkey/stock.adobe.com; page 107 (b) © Shutterstock/Lukas Gojda; page 111 © JulesSelmes2014; page 113 © B4Step/Fotolia.com; page 121 © Jacob Crees Cockayne; page 125 © Somwaya/stock.adobe.com; page 128 © Bojan/stock.adobe.com; page 129 © Anyka - Fotolia; page 137 © zinkevych/stock.adobe.com; page 138 © Cozine/stock.adobe.com; page 139 © sam74100 - 123RF; page 141 (t) © helix/Fotolia.com, (b) © fox17/Fotolia.com; page 142 © The Eatwell Guide/Gov.UK/Crown Copyright; page 145 © dalaprod - Fotolia; page 150 © hitdelight/Fotolia.com; page 151 © Monkey Business/Fotolia.com; page 153 © rebecca abell/Fotolia.com; page 155 © Rawpixel.com/stock.adobe.com; page 156 © Roger Ressmeyer/Corbis/VCG via Getty Images; page 157 © Irochka/Fotolia.com; page 161 © Stocksnapper/Fotolia.com; page 163 (both) © JulesSelmes2014; page 164 © Stefan Andronache/Fotolia.com; page 165 © JulesSelmes2014; page 168 © wckiw/stock.adobe.com; page 169 © Jacob Crees Cockayne.

Guide to the book

What you will learn in this unit
Appearing at the beginning of each chapter, this box tells you what you will learn in the chapter.

Important words
These boxes explain the meaning of the words you will need to know for the qualification.

Example!
These boxes will give you examples of what is being discussed on the page.

Task
These boxes suggest things you can do to help you to understand the subjects that have been explained on the page. For example, you may be asked to discuss the subjects in pairs or as part of a group.

Assessment task
These boxes describe work which, if completed, will contribute towards your Evidence Record, which will allow you to pass the qualification.

Case study
These boxes give an example of a real person or situation that helps illustrate the point in the chapter.

Summary
This box appears at the end of each chapter, and reminds you of what you should have learnt from reading the chapter.

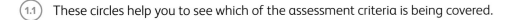 (1.1) These circles help you to see which of the assessment criteria is being covered.

Chapter 1

CFC 13 Sharing learning experiences with children

What you will learn in this unit

You will gain an understanding of:

◆ the ways in which children learn
◆ how to use stories and rhymes with young children
◆ how exploring the natural world can support children's learning
◆ ways in which the local community can give children different experiences.

LO1 How children learn

1.1 Ways that children learn

Observation

When children watch what is happening around them, they are observing. Children like to **observe** what other children are doing and this can help them to learn new things. They will often watch other children playing a game or doing an activity, and perhaps want to join in.

Children like to watch adults doing tasks, such as cooking the dinner, baking a cake or putting on make-up. They will often copy what they have seen by using role play.

Important words

Observe – look at or watch.

Task

In pairs, discuss when you have learnt how to do something by watching other people. Why do you think observing was the best way to learn?

Experimenting

This is when children do tests (**experiments**) to see how things work, what things do or what might happen. Children like to test their own skills to see if they can do things that they have seen others do, for example, skipping or rolling a toy car down a ramp.

Children may **experiment** by dropping objects into water to see if they float or sink to the bottom. During bath time, children often experiment with bubbles or floating toys.

When playing outside, children may enjoy jumping in puddles of water to see how far the water spreads out. They often also do this to assess the reactions of others around them and this helps with their social development.

> ## Important words
>
> **An experiment** – a test to see how something works or what might happen.
>
> **Experiment** – test or try out new things.

Figure 1.1 Children may enjoy jumping in puddles to see how the water splashes

Imaginative and creative play

This happens when children use their own imagination to create a make-believe world. For example, children sometimes pretend to be other people, such as a doctor, a police officer or a shop assistant. Children often enjoy dressing up to look like a character, such as a pirate or a princess. It is usual to observe children acting out a story they have listened to, perhaps using small characters or toys. They may also make up their own stories or create little scenes,

Task

Talk about when you have seen a child using their imagination or being creative. Perhaps the child was pretending to be a character, or they were retelling a story they had listened to, or perhaps they were being creative with crayons or paints.

for example, using teddies to play at being a school teacher or arranging jungle animals to pretend to be at the zoo.

Some children enjoy being creative with dough or clay. They have the chance to make models or shapes, or simply enjoy exploring the squishy texture using their senses. When painting during a messy play session, some children really enjoy using a wide range of paints and this is a good opportunity for them to use their own imagination to create a picture just as they want it to look.

Figure 1.2 Playdough can encourage children to use their imagination

1.2 How children use their senses to explore the world

Sense	How the sense is used
Sight	Children use sight to observe the world around them, to see what everything looks like, e.g. children quickly learn to recognise people, objects and places.
Hearing	Children listen to and recognise sounds, e.g. a very young baby will recognise the voice of their main carer. Older children can identify animals through the noise they make.
Touch	Children **investigate** using touch to find out what things feel like. By touching, children can experience different textures, e.g. some children may not like the texture of sand or seaweed under their feet when they are walking on the beach.

Table 1.1 How children use their **senses** to explore

Sense	How the sense is used
Smell	Children use this sense to experience pleasant or unpleasant smells, e.g. children may recognise what is cooking by the smell in the air, or a person by the perfume they wear.
Taste	Children use their sense of taste to discover different flavours, e.g. some children like sweet tastes while others prefer spicy foods.

Table 1.1 How children use their senses to explore *(Continued)*

Important words

Investigate – find out (about something).

Senses – sight, hearing, touch, smell and taste: used to make sense of the world around us.

Task

Josh is going to the supermarket with his grandpa.

In pairs, discuss and list the ways that Josh will use his senses to investigate how things look, smell and feel in the supermarket.

For example, Josh might use his sense of sight to look at the different colours on the packets and boxes.

Assessment task 1

Design a poster to show how children use their senses to find out about the world around them. Include sight, hearing, touch, smell and taste in your poster. The poster should show three reasons why it is important for children to find out about the world around them.

1.3 The importance of investigation for children's learning

Children learn by investigating the world around them. They do this by using all of their senses.

Children need lots of opportunities to learn through investigation. Often children will investigate on their own, without the help of an adult.

However, children may need adults around them to provide a wide range of opportunities to investigate, such as giving them wet and dry sand to see and feel the difference. Children could discover that if the sand is too wet, it will be difficult to make a sandcastle because the sand will not

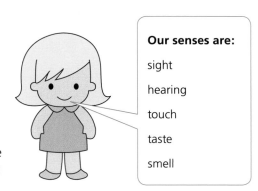

Our senses are:

sight

hearing

touch

taste

smell

Figure 1.3 Children learn through their senses

come out of the bucket easily. If the sand is too dry, it will not stick together and hold its shape, so the sand needs to be slightly wet.

Children learn more when they try things out for themselves rather than observing other people doing activities or watching the television.

Example!
Aadi will enjoy watching Josh completing a jigsaw puzzle, but will learn more about shape and size by trying to fit the pieces of the jigsaw together by himself.

Children learn by using their senses to investigate the world around them. Through investigation children learn how things work, what things do and why things happen. Children discover for themselves the best way to do things, such as the best way to carry a bucket of water without spilling the water is to carry the bucket carefully, keeping the bucket level.

Children may learn how to keep themselves safe through investigation: a child could learn that if they walk along a log or wooden beam, they must tread carefully to help them balance.

Through investigation children learn about living things, such as how fish swim in water, how a frog jumps or how plants and flowers grow.

Figure 1.4 By investigating, children learn how things work

LO2 Sharing stories and rhymes

Most children love listening to stories. They often have a favourite story and favourite characters from the stories they have listened to. Many stories and rhymes enjoyed by young children can support their learning. Adults can use **sensory aids** with the rhymes and stories to encourage children to join in. Table 1.2 gives examples of sensory aids or props to use with different rhymes and stories, so that children are encouraged to take part in the activity.

Important words

Sensory aid – objects or materials used by children to encourage the use of their senses when learning.

2.1, 2.2, 2.3 Stories and rhymes, sensory aids and ways to encourage taking part

Story or rhyme	Sensory aids	Ways to encourage children to take part
Handa's Surprise	◆ A basket full of the fruit used in the story ◆ Animal masks ◆ A map of the country in Africa (Kenya) that Handa lives	Children can touch, smell and taste the fruit, learning the names of the fruit and where each one grows. Children can enjoy pretending to be the animals in the story. The map can be used to show where the story takes place. The children can learn new things about a different country. These aids can be left in the role-play area to encourage children to retell the story later.
The Very Hungry Caterpillar by Eric Carle	◆ A storyboard showing the life cycle of a butterfly, e.g. caterpillar hatches and eats a lot of food, then caterpillar slowly changes into a beautiful butterfly that flies away. ◆ Pictures of food or actual food the caterpillar might enjoy.	Children can use the storyboard to see the life cycle of a butterfly. Children can taste and smell the food to see which they think the caterpillar would enjoy most.

Table 1.2 Using sensory aids to support children's learning

Story or rhyme	Sensory aids	Ways to encourage children to take part
Twinkle, Twinkle, Little Star 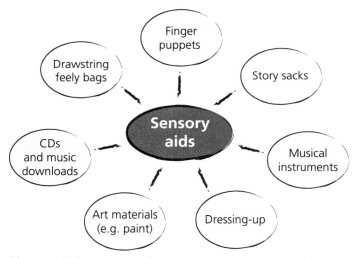	◆ Different shapes in a feely box or drawstring bag ◆ A range of materials: silky, shiny, sparkly, glittery ◆ A collection of musical instruments	Put the shapes in a box or bag and ask the children to close their eyes, feel the shapes and pick out a star shape. Give children the materials, encourage them to investigate the textures and describe what they all feel like. Share out the instruments and enable children to experiment with bells and chimes.
Old McDonald had a Farm	◆ Different animal noises: on a CD, download or online ◆ Animal glove puppets	Play the sounds and see if the children can recognise each animal sound. Use the glove puppets at appropriate points in the song alongside the animal sounds.

Table 1.2 Using sensory aids to support children's learning *(Continued)*

Figure 1.5 items around central "Sensory aids": Finger puppets, Drawstring feely bags, Story sacks, CDs and music downloads, Musical instruments, Art materials (e.g. paint), Dressing-up.

Figure 1.5 Examples of sensory aids to support play and learning

Task

Look at Figure 1.5, which shows examples of sensory aids that can be used to support play and learning. Can you think of any other sensory aids that could be used?

Children might like to re-enact a story using dressing-up clothes and props in the role-play area. Children may listen to a story on a tablet and then act out this story using items around them. For example, after listening to *Goldilocks and the Three Bears* children might use cuddly toys to play the role of the bears. Children might create pictures they have seen or imagined from a story, using paints and crayons. When investigating outdoors, children may come across objects or living things that they have only read about in books before.

Younger children enjoy hearing the same nursery rhyme or song over and over again, and soon begin to join in with some of the words or actions. After hearing the same rhyme many times, children begin to remember all the words for themselves.

Task

In small groups:
1 Choose a story that Stephanie, who is four and a half years old, and Jake, who is three years old, might enjoy.
2 Draw a spider diagram of all the sensory aids which would support the children's enjoyment and learning of the story.

Assessment task 2

Look back at Table 1.2. Copy one story or rhyme from the table and then add one of your own. Remember to include the sensory aids (equipment) you could use, and how you could encourage children to take part.

LO3 Exploring the natural environment

There are many learning opportunities for children when investigating and exploring the natural world. There are many places that adults can take children to learn about the natural environment and to develop the children's **curiosity**. Children are usually naturally curious. They will want to look and touch things that they have not seen before, so it is very important to think about keeping them safe and out of danger when we take them out on visits.

Some children have lots of opportunities to explore the local environment, but children who live in crowded cities or large towns with no green spaces may not have safe outdoor spaces near to where they live.

3.1 Objects of interest

Because children are very curious, they will often pick up and explore objects that they find in the **natural environment**. Again, it is important that the adult makes sure that these objects are safe for children to touch and that children are not harmed when exploring.

Handling objects is a very good way to learn about the environment. Children can examine objects, such as shells and pinecones, by using all their senses. Some children may only have ever seen these objects before in books or on television.

Important words

Curiosity – interest that is shown to learn new things or gain knowledge.

Natural environment – green spaces, which may be planted with trees, contain rivers or be used as parks.

Task

Think of some items that could harm children if they were found in an outdoor space.

3.2 Natural environments

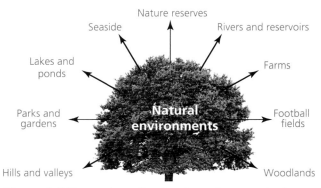

Figure 1.6 Examples of natural environments for children to explore

Nature reserves
Seaside
Rivers and reservoirs
Lakes and ponds
Farms
Parks and gardens
Natural environments
Football fields
Hills and valleys
Woodlands

Figure 1.7 There are many new things to learn at the seaside

3.3 Outdoor experiences to develop children's curiosity

Figure 1.7 shows a young child at the seaside. Some of the things a child may learn in this environment are:

◆ what lives in rock pools
◆ what shells look and feel like and what kind of creature lived in them
◆ how the sand feels under their feet
◆ how the texture of the sand changes nearer to the seashore
◆ what seaweed looks and smells like
◆ what the sea sounds like.

Assessment task 3

In small groups, discuss a natural environment in your area.

Copy Table 1.3 and fill in the blank cells. Add another natural environment in the final row and fill in the details about the objects of interest that can be found there and what children can learn. Think about any possible dangers to children that might be found in this natural environment.

The natural environment	Objects of interest	What children can learn
By the seaside	◆ Shells ◆ Sea creatures ◆ Seaweed ◆ Driftwood ◆ Pebbles	What shells look and feel like and which sea creatures lived in them; what seaweed looks and smells like; how driftwood and pebbles are shaped by the force of the sea.

Table 1.3 What children can learn from the natural world

CACHE Level 1 Caring for Children

The natural environment	Objects of interest	What children can learn
In a woodland		
In a local park		
(Add another natural environment that you can think of.)		

Table 1.3 What children can learn from the natural world *(Continued)*

LO4 Community

4.1 Examples of different community organisations

Examples of different community organisations include:

- Sure Start
- local children's centres
- local library for books and toys
- swimming clubs
- toddler groups
- Tumble Tots
- dance classes
- football coaching
- gymnastic clubs
- rap and rhyme
- indoor soft-play centres
- adventure playgrounds
- messy or sensory play workshops

4.2 How local organisations can broaden children's experiences

There are many organisations, services and people who can help to provide experiences for children in the local area. The community or community organisations can provide environments that enable children to try new things, learn skills and enjoy themselves.

Different services can give children the chance to widen their experiences and learn new skills by providing them with activities to take part in. Some new experiences for them may be messy play sessions, football coaching or gymnastics classes.

Important words

Broaden children's experiences – giving children the opportunity to take part in a wide range of activities or experiences, locally and within the wider environment.

Assessment task 4

List four services in the community. Discuss and write two benefits to children of taking part in each of these four services. (For example, by taking part in a dance class, young children will learn about music and movement. They will be improving their gross motor skills and co-ordination. They may also make new friends and gain confidence.)

Summary

In this unit you have learnt that:

◆ children can learn in many ways and use their senses to do this

◆ children enjoy investigating and finding out about the world they live in

◆ adults need to make sure they keep children safe when they are investigating the world around them

◆ children enjoy stories and rhymes, and when encouraged by adults, children can learn lots of new things through books

◆ children are very interested in natural objects, and will enjoy looking at, feeling, smelling and listening to all kinds of natural objects when they are outdoors

◆ children might enjoy taking part in activities and services provided for them within their local community.

What you will learn in this unit

You will gain an understanding of:

◆ the growth and development of children from birth to five years and 11 months
◆ different factors (issues) which affect growth and development
◆ the importance of a good diet and exercise for children's growth and development
◆ activities to support children's physical development
◆ ways to support children's language skills
◆ ways to encourage children to play socially (with other people and children).

Growth and development

Babies and children not only grow bigger in size as they get older, but they also go through what are known as '**stages of development**'. From birth, how babies look and what they can do changes very quickly.

◆ **Growth** is about the body growing and getting bigger in size and weight, for example, children grow taller and their feet get bigger. Growth happens naturally if children are healthy and well cared for.
◆ **Development** is about learning new skills, such as learning to talk, remembering the names of colours or learning how to kick a ball. Children need lots of different activities and the support of adults to develop new skills.

Important words

Patterns or stages of development – when a baby or child develops a skill and can then move on to develop another more difficult skill. For example, the next stage of development for a baby who can stand will be to walk while holding onto an adult's hand.

LO1 Factors that can affect children's growth and development up to 5 months 11 years

Milestones of development tell us about the skills that children might have at a certain age. All children are different and grow at different rates. We must remember that not all children will follow these milestones, for example, some children learn to speak at a very young age, but might not be able to run and jump so soon.

1.1 The stages of development of children from birth to six years

Babies from birth to three months				
Physical development	**Intellectual development**	**Language development**	**Emotional development**	**Social development**
Sleeps for around 18 hours each day. Feeds every two to three hours during the day and will need to be fed less often during the night.	Begins to use senses to hear, smell and see what is going on around them.	At first a baby is only able to cry, but quickly learns to make cooing and gurgling sounds. Babies are soothed by the sound of familiar voices.	A baby will cry when in pain, hungry or uncomfortable, such as when they have a wet nappy or feel too hot or cold.	A newborn baby will try to look at faces, especially when they are being fed. By the age of three months a baby may copy an adult's smile.
Babies aged three to six months				
Physical development	**Intellectual development**	**Language development**	**Emotional development**	**Social development**
Feeds three to five times every day. The baby can control head and arm movements, such as grasping a toy or rolling over on a play mat.	Greater development of senses: a baby will turn towards a sound and learn who different people are by listening to their voice or looking at their face.	A baby will make many different sounds, such as babbling and cooing when they are enjoying a bath, or grunting and crying when they are unhappy or tired.	Enjoys being cuddled and rocked.	Knows the difference between family members. Usually enjoys contact with family members, such as when feeding and being bathed.

Table 2.1 Developmental stages from birth to six years

Babies aged six to 12 months (one year)				
Physical development	**Intellectual development**	**Language development**	**Emotional development**	**Social development**
Eats three meals and two snacks every day. Sleeps for around 12 hours every night and may have two naps a day. Begins to control own body and hands by moving objects or pulling things towards them. At around eight months, a baby will begin to sit without support, and may start to crawl.	Enjoys playing: moves toys and objects from one place to another so that by the time the baby is 12 months old, they are able to stack one brick onto another. Babies enjoy looking at bright colours.	Babies easily recognise the people around them by the sound of their voice and enjoy listening to songs and rhymes. By 12 months, a baby might say one or two words and copy some sounds.	Babies may become clingy to family members because they are now more aware of strangers.	Gives and takes objects or toys. May wave bye-bye. By 12 months, babies have learned to look when someone calls their name and might understand some simple requests.
Children aged one to two years				
Physical development	**Intellectual development**	**Language development**	**Emotional development**	**Social development**
Stands without support and begins to walk. Can climb up stairs, so needs to be watched! By the age of two years, a child can run, throw and kick a ball.	Begins to make lines on paper with crayons or paints. By the age of two years, a child may enjoy building a tower of two bricks and pushing them over.	Children begin to repeat a few words and understand some instructions, such as 'coat on', 'come here'. Understands about 50 words at two years of age.	A child may be interested in looking at themselves in the mirror, such as when clapping or pulling faces.	Enjoys simple clapping games, such as pat-a-cake. Enjoys feeding themselves.

Table 2.1 Developmental stages from birth to six years *(Continued)*

Children aged two to three years				
Physical development	**Intellectual development**	**Language development**	**Emotional development**	**Social development**
Learns to jump off a low step and may ride a tricycle. Uses a spoon and fork properly when feeding themselves. May take an interest in using the toilet or potty.	Uses crayons to draw in circular movements and make simple shapes. May enjoy dough and messy activities. They can also build higher towers by balancing more bricks. Enjoys listening to others count and may begin to join in.	A child will put three or four more words together to make sentences: for example, 'me do that mummy' or 'little dog bark'. Children will learn lots of new words and enjoy looking at picture books and listening to stories. Understands over 600 words by the age of three years.	A child may be worried when family members leave them; the child may cry when starting nursery or if the parent goes out for the evening, leaving the child with a babysitter. Understands the meaning of different facial expressions, for example, children will know when a person is happy or sad.	Uses 'I', 'me' and 'you'. Copies actions, such as when singing rhymes at nursery. Copies adults' actions by pretending to clean the car or stir food in a pan. Can dislike sharing with others. Children at this age may enjoy playing next to other children but may not play with them. Enjoys routines: a child may look forward to getting up and going to nursery every morning or sharing a bedtime story each evening.

Table 2.1 Developmental stages from birth to six years *(Continued)*

Children aged three to four years				
Physical development	**Intellectual development**	**Language development**	**Emotional development**	**Social development**
Stands on one leg, jumps up and down. Enjoys climbing and can change direction quickly when running in the play area. May now be able to take responsibility for their own toileting.	Draws circles with more control and may add lines for arms and legs or dots for eyes. Can count up to ten and begins to learn the names of colours and shapes.	Understands over 1,000 words and makes sentences of four or five words. Children now enjoy listening to longer stories and will often choose the same story over and over again.	Shows a sense of humour: may tell jokes and make funny faces or do funny walks. Likes to spend time playing alone but also enjoys playing with other children. May enjoy hugs and cuddles with family and friends.	Gives orders. Enjoys playing with other children and will leave the main carer more easily, such as when going to nursery.
Children aged four to five years 11 months				
Physical development	**Intellectual development**	**Language development**	**Emotional development**	**Social development**
Can open and close fastenings: can dress and undress for a PE lesson. Can use scissors to cut out shapes and pictures. Skips with a rope. Runs quickly and safely around the playground without bumping into other children. Is able to use a variety of large equipment, such as swings and slides. Can throw a football and can sometimes catch it.	Can copy letters and numbers and write their own name. Draws pictures of trees, houses, people and animals. Can complete a 20-piece jigsaw puzzle.	Children at this age know up to 2,000 words and can form proper sentences. Children often talk clearly and will enjoy telling stories about themselves.	Enjoys caring for pets. Shows concern when a friend is hurt. Children will like to make choices for themselves, such as deciding which clothes to wear or which book to look at.	Children are now more able to do things for themselves, such as wiping up spilled juice. They may also like to help other children, such as helping a younger child to complete a jigsaw. Children at this age usually enjoy being busy and playing cooperatively. This means that they can agree rules of a game and take turns.

Table 2.1 Developmental stages from birth to six years (Continued)

1.2 Factors that affect growth and development

Illness

Illness can affect a child's growth and development. Some illnesses can mean that a child may not grow as quickly as other children of the same age.

Task

Working in pairs or small groups, write down the differences between a newborn baby and a child aged four years. Think about what the four-year-old might be able to do compared to the newborn baby.

Illness affects a child's development because when they are ill, they may not feel well enough to exercise or play with other children. They may spend time in hospital or not be able to go to school with their friends. Children might have to take medicines or need medical treatments that can make them feel unwell, tired or miserable. This may mean a child does not get to learn new things.

Disability or impairment

Disability or impairment may be something that can be seen, such as wearing glasses or using a wheelchair, or it can be something that is invisible, such as a heart condition or **autism**. It may affect a child's development if they are not given the correct support from adults. For example, a child who needs glasses (due to a visual impairment) may not be able to see pictures in a book or see a computer screen clearly without their glasses.

Important words ❗

Autism – a condition that affects how a child develops, communicates and relates to other people and how they experience the world around them.

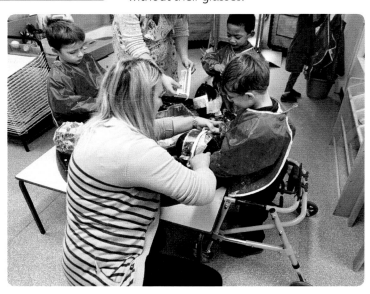

Figure 2.1 Adults need to make sure all children can enjoy taking part in activities

However, if a child who uses a wheelchair, for instance, is given the correct support, they should be able to enjoy most activities with other children. Adults who care for children must think about how to plan activities to make sure that all children can join in, for example, arranging the tables to ensure that a child who uses a wheelchair has space to move around safely.

Lifestyle

The lifestyle of a child and their family can have a good or bad effect on the child's development. For example, if adults smoke in the house, close to where the child is sleeping or playing, the child could develop breathing difficulties. If the family does not choose to exercise or spend time doing activities outdoors, the child's health and physical development may be affected. If the family does not have a good bedtime routine, the child may become unwell or be too tired to join in with activities and could miss out on learning new things.

1.3 The importance of diet and exercise

Diet

To stay healthy, children need a good, well-balanced diet. This should include plenty of healthy fruit, vegetables, dairy and proteins, such as fish or beans. These foods will help to support children's healthy growth and development.

A poor diet might mean that children do not get all the vitamins and nutrients their bodies need. It often means that children eat a lot of food which contains too much salt, fat or sugar. This can cause health problems, such as diabetes or becoming overweight.

Exercise

Children naturally like to run and move around. They need opportunities to exercise so they can build strong muscles and develop skills, such as balance and co-ordination.

Exercise gives children the chance to build up their **stamina**, for example, running without feeling out of breath. Exercise can also help children to feel mentally happier and healthier.

Not enough exercise might cause children's muscles to become weak. They may build up too much body fat and become ill later in life. Children who do not exercise can become less interested in the world around them. All children need to have ample opportunities to enjoy exercising in many different ways.

Task

In pairs, write down three different ways in which children can take part in exercise. For example, playing with a frisbee.

Important words

Stamina – ability to keep going for a long time, for example with exercise.

Figure 2.2 Growth and development can be measured

2.1, 2.2, 2.3 Activities to promote physical and social development, communication and language skills

As long as children are given food and water and their basic care needs are met, their bodies will usually grow taller and heavier.

However, in order for children to develop physically, they need more than food and water. Children need to be able to socialise with others and to be communicated with to support their language development. They need to be involved in activities which are suitable for their age and stage of development. They also need toys and equipment to play with, such as tricycles and scooters, or bricks and plastic cups to stack. Children need to have opportunities to explore, play and socialise with other children in a safe environment. Adults can provide the appropriate equipment and also make sure that the children are enjoying the activity and are safe and well supervised.

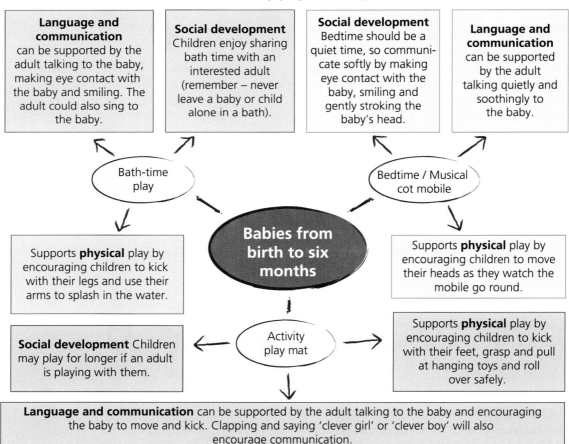

Language and communication can be supported by the adult talking to the baby, making eye contact with the baby and smiling. The adult could also sing to the baby.

Social development Children enjoy sharing bath time with an interested adult (remember – never leave a baby or child alone in a bath).

Social development Bedtime should be a quiet time, so communicate softly by making eye contact with the baby, smiling and gently stroking the baby's head.

Language and communication can be supported by the adult talking quietly and soothingly to the baby.

Bath-time play

Bedtime / Musical cot mobile

Babies from birth to six months

Supports **physical** play by encouraging children to kick with their legs and use their arms to splash in the water.

Supports **physical** play by encouraging children to move their heads as they watch the mobile go round.

Activity play mat

Supports **physical** play by encouraging children to kick with their feet, grasp and pull at hanging toys and roll over safely.

Social development Children may play for longer if an adult is playing with them.

Language and communication can be supported by the adult talking to the baby and encouraging the baby to move and kick. Clapping and saying 'clever girl' or 'clever boy' will also encourage communication.

Figure 2.3 How activities support babies' physical development, social and emotional development and language and communication skills, from birth to six months

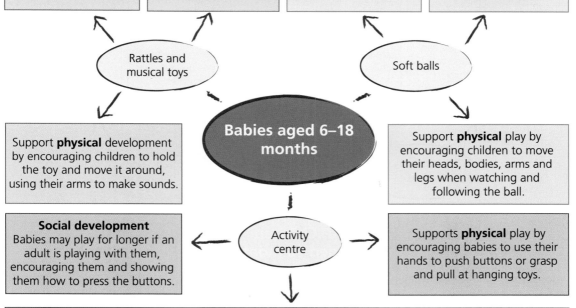

Language and communication can be supported by the adult encouraging the child through talking and praising the child's efforts. The adult could also sing along to the sounds the child makes.

Social development Babies and young children will enjoy the company of an adult or older child when making sounds with musical toys.

Social development When the child is with other children, ball play is a good way to introduce turn-taking and sharing.

Language and communication can be supported by the adult giving encouragement to the child to 'catch it, roll it, kick it' and by saying 'well done' or 'that's clever!'

Rattles and musical toys

Soft balls

Babies aged 6–18 months

Support **physical** development by encouraging children to hold the toy and move it around, using their arms to make sounds.

Support **physical** play by encouraging children to move their heads, bodies, arms and legs when watching and following the ball.

Social development Babies may play for longer if an adult is playing with them, encouraging them and showing them how to press the buttons.

Activity centre

Supports **physical** play by encouraging babies to use their hands to push buttons or grasp and pull at hanging toys.

Language and communication can be supported by the adult talking to the baby and using words such as 'push, pull, press', encouraging them by saying 'you do it'. Clapping and saying 'clever girl' or 'clever boy' will also encourage communication.

Figure 2.4 How activities support babies' physical development, social and emotional development and language and communication skills, from six to 18 months

Task

In small groups, think about other activities for each of the age groups. Write down how they might support a child's physical development, social and emotional development, and language and communication skills.

Task

Write down ways in which adults can support children to learn more from these activities.

Language and communication can be supported by the adult encouraging the child to count the steps as they climb to the top. They can also use language to describe the child's actions; for example: 'climb up, high, slippery, whooosh'.

Social development Young children will get an understanding of taking turns when they climb the steps of the slide. Children often enjoy watching other children slide down, even if they are unsure about having a go.

Social development Up to the age of three, children will watch other children play but will not always play together.

Language and communication can be supported by the adult giving encouragement to the child to 'hold on'. Language such as 'backwards' and 'forwards' could be used.

Outdoor slide

Sit-and-ride toys

Children aged 18 months to three years

Supports **physical** development by giving children the opportunity to climb, balance, slide and jump.

Support **physical** play by encouraging children to move their arms to steer the bike and their legs to balance and move the bike along.

Social development Young children enjoy painting and drawing with other children and adults. They like to watch what other people create and have new ideas of their own.

Painting and drawing

Support **physical development** by encouraging children to use their hands to hold the pencil or brush. They will also practise controlling the pencil to make shapes or lines on the paper.

Language and communication can be supported by the adult talking to the child about what they are drawing or painting. This could be about the shapes they are making, the colours they are using and the way in which paints mix together on the paper.

Figure 2.5 How activities support children's physical development, social and emotional development and language and communication skills, from three to six year

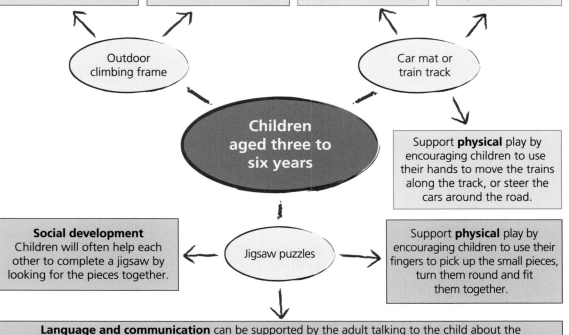

Language and communication can be supported by the adult talking to the child about the picture on the jigsaw.

Figure 2.6 How activities support children's physical development, social and emotional development and language and communication skills, from three to six years

Assessment task

Using some of the ideas in Figures 2.4, 2.5 and 2.6, make three information cards, one for each of these age groups:
- six to 18 months
- 18 months to three years
- three to six years.

Look at the sample information card shown in Figure 2.7, for a baby aged 0–6 months. Make sure that your information cards give ideas for supporting the growth and development of young children, as in this example.

Information card

Bath time for babies 0–6 months

Physical development can be supported by the adult encouraging the child to kick with their legs and use their arms to splash in the water.

Social development can be supported by an interested adult playing with the baby at bath time.

Language and communication can be supported by the adult talking to the baby, making eye contact with the baby and smiling. The adult could also sing to the baby.

Figure 2.7 Example of an information card

Summary

In this unit you have learnt that:

◆ there are stages of children's growth and development from birth to five years 11 months

◆ factors (issues) can affect growth and development, such as diet and exercise

◆ different activities can support children's growth and development.

What you will learn in this unit

You will gain an understanding of:

◆ stages of growth and development that people go through

◆ factors that may affect physical growth and development

◆ effects of ageing later on in life.

Important words

Wellbeing – health.

Emotional and social wellbeing – happiness in yourself and as part of a group (society).

Case study

Grace is 82 years old. She lives alone because her partner died two years ago. Grace has lived an active life but has recently experienced a stroke, so she has had to spend a few weeks in her local hospital. She has made some good progress and, as she is getting better, she is hoping to leave the hospital soon to go home.

Grace's daughter lives nearby, so she will help Grace by cooking her food and doing jobs around the house.

Before Grace leaves the hospital, a specialist nurse must consider how well Grace will be able to manage at home. She needs to find out about Grace's physical, intellectual, **emotional and social wellbeing**.

Grace has enjoyed swimming all her life and swam twice a week in the local pool as a child and throughout her life until she reached 74 years of age. Grace has always made sure that she eats a good, balanced diet. She admitted to smoking for a couple of years during her teenage years. However, she realised it was unhealthy and soon stopped.

She caught measles when she was seven years old, which made her very ill. Grace has slight hearing loss in one ear because of this illness.

The happiest times in Grace's life were when she married Bob, her partner, and when her children were born. The time when Grace was most sad was when her partner died; she then had to live alone. Another difficult time for Grace was when she experienced the stroke. This made her very frightened and worried about how she would look after herself in the future.

This case study will be referred to later in this chapter.

LO1 Human growth and development

1.1 Main stages of human growth and development

People move through different stages of growth and development during their lives. When we are talking about a person's lifetime, we can look at five important 'life stages', which are shown in Figure 3.1.

Infancy   Childhood   Adolescence   Adulthood   Older adulthood

Figure 3.1 A timeline of the different life stages

Infancy

This is the time between birth and five years. It is a time when young children need their families to provide everything they require, such as food and drink and meeting their social and communication needs as they are not able to care for themselves yet. Although some children at this age will not be at school, they are still learning at a very fast rate. During this time, children change from being a tiny baby to a school-aged child who can walk, talk and begin to care for themselves.

Childhood

This is the time in a child's life when they start full-time school and begin to have their own friends. The stage of childhood begins at the age of five and continues until a child is about 12 years old. Again, growth and development are happening quickly and a child changes very much during this stage. Adults should enable the child to try to do more things for themselves, such as helping them to wash and dress themselves, so that as they get older children can learn to care for themselves.

Adolescence

This stage in a person's life begins at around 12 or 13 years of age, as they become a teenager. During this stage, the body goes through many physical changes which are linked to reproduction (having babies). Hormone changes inside the body can affect growth, mood and appearance. Some teenagers find this stage of their life quite difficult, but most of this will have disappeared as they reach adulthood.

Adulthood

When people move into adulthood, they may have a job, a partner and perhaps even a family of their own to care for. Physical growth and development have stopped, and later in adulthood the body begins to show signs of ageing, for example, some adults may not be able to run as fast or climb as many stairs as they used to. However, social and emotional changes are still happening at this stage and the brain is still working very well.

Figure 3.2 Older adulthood brings many challenges, but it can also be a happy and fulfilling time of life

Task

In small groups, think about an older person that you know (it could be a neighbour or grandparent). Discuss the effects that ageing has had on this person.

You could also write down ways that family or friends could help this older person to continue to safely care for themselves. For example, having handrails fitted for outdoor steps.

Older adulthood (2.3)

During this life stage, people are more likely to become ill or physically less able. This is because a person's body is getting weaker, particularly if they did not take care of their bodies when they were teenagers and adults. If we smoke or drink too much alcohol, it could damage our bodies.

During this life stage, skin begins to lose elasticity so will become lined. Hair will lose its colour and become grey. Muscles weaken, so walking may become slower and tasks that were once easy, are now difficult.

Some older people might have sight or hearing loss. They may live alone after the death of a partner and their family may not live nearby, so they may become lonely. However, older adults often have lots of wisdom and experience of the world and enjoy their lives very much.

Assessment task 1

Refer to the case study on pages 25–6. Make a poster to show:
- a **pathway** of Grace's life. Remember to include all five stages. Use pictures from magazines or draw what a person at each stage will look like
- a brief description of the effects of ageing that Grace may have experienced during older adulthood
- what is meant by physical, intellectual, emotional and social development. Use the information below to help you.

Important words

Pathway – a timeline.

1.2 What are physical, intellectual, emotional and social development?

Physical development

This means the way in which bodies grow and how people develop physical skills. A baby learns to walk, a child will be developing new skills, such as balancing, catching a ball or learning to draw, and a teenager might run quickly and jump over objects. Adults mostly use the skills they have but sometimes learn new or more difficult skills, such as rock climbing. As we move into older adulthood, physical skills or activities may become more difficult, for instance, running. As they age, some older adults may need a cane or stick to support them when walking.

Intellectual development

This is the way in which our brain develops and works. As we go through the different life stages, our brain takes in more information that we can understand and use. Babies are born not knowing much but quickly learn from the people and the world around them. Most children learn to read and write, so can understand more and communicate with others to get more information about the world. Adults continue to learn and use their knowledge and understanding in their work. However, as we move through older adulthood, the brain may start to slow down and people can become forgetful or confused.

Emotional development

This is the development of many emotions, such as anxiety and fear or excitement and joy. During each life stage, people have different emotions to deal with. Experiencing or feeling these emotions is completely normal. We are usually aware of why we might feel these emotions, such as feeling confident or nervous when meeting new people or excited at being given or giving someone a present. Children and adults need to develop **resilience** to deal with emotions as these are all part of life.

Social development

This is about understanding the needs of others as well as your own, within social relationships. It is also understanding how to behave in different places. For example, children need to know how to behave towards teachers and their friends in school, and teenagers have more independence and need to behave in a more mature way. Children and teenagers need to understand that they can cause others to be upset or worried if they are unkind to each other, but they can also help others to feel good about themselves if they show kindness and support. Older adults might lose partners or friends that they spent time with, so to stop them becoming lonely they may find new ways to socialise.

Task

Think about the emotions that a child starting school might feel. Write down ways in which an adult can help the child to cope with this new experience.

Example!

A young child might be upset if they lose a favourite toy. A teenager may worry about exams or friendships, whereas an adult may worry about household bills. An older adult may feel annoyed if they cannot do something which they found easy to do when they were younger.

LO2 Factors affecting growth and development

2.1 Factors affecting physical growth and development

As a person goes through the life stages from birth to older adulthood, there are many factors which may affect their physical growth, such as exercise, diet, lifestyle or illness. (See Chapter 16, HL 1 Healthy living, for more information about factors affecting growth and development.)

Important words

Resilience – being able to cope with a situation or feeling.

Factors affecting physical growth and development – negative or positive experiences that change how we grow or develop.

2.2 Life events which can affect emotional and social wellbeing

There are certain times in a person's life that can affect their emotional and social wellbeing. Good experiences that can make an adult feel happy may include a birth in the family, getting married, getting a good job or moving to a new house. There could also be times in an adult's life when they feel sad or very worried, such as losing a home or a job, a family splitting up or the death of a close family member.

Figure 3.3 A wedding is an important life event

Important words

Circumstances or life events – situations or experiences in a person's life.

Task

Think about different factors or events that have affected your physical health and experiences, and your emotional and social wellbeing.

Assessment task 2

Think about the case study on pages 25–6.
Using what you have learnt about Grace:
- list three factors which may have affected her physical health and development during her lifetime
- list three experiences in Grace's life which may have affected her emotional and social wellbeing.

Summary

In this unit you have learnt that:
- there are five main life stages
- factors such as diet, lifestyle and exercise can affect physical growth and development
- events such as the birth of a child or the death of a close family member are called 'life events'
- life events can affect a person's social and emotional wellbeing.

What you will learn in this unit

You will gain an understanding of:

◆ how to respect and value children as individuals
◆ why it is important to value children as individuals
◆ ways to respect and value children
◆ the rights of children.

LO1 Respect and value children as individuals

1.1 How to respect and value children as individuals

Every baby, child, teenager and adult is different. Children are all individuals and like different things. They may also have very different **lifestyles** and cultural backgrounds (including different religions, eating habits and how they are expected to behave at home). They may have different living conditions or live with different parents/carers. For example, a child may live with just their father, or there may be three or four children living with their mum and their grandparents. Some children may live in a caravan within a community of travellers; others may spend time with foster carers if there is a difficulty in the family, such as a parent or primary carer who has had to go into hospital. Some children have disabilities or other individual needs.

Children are all very different, but every child has the right to grow up feeling happy and loved.

Important words !

Lifestyle – the ways in which a person lives their life and the choices which they make.

Task

Look at the picture of the friends in Figure 4.1. They are all very different. In small groups, write down some of the things that make you or people in your families individual.

1.2 Why adults should value and respect children

It is very important for all adults to treat everyone with respect, as children look at the way in which adults behave and copy their behaviour.

Important words

Respecting children – this is when you feel and behave positively towards children.

Figure 4.1 We all have individual appearances

Example!

If adults talk kindly to children and listen to what they say, the children will feel important and will learn that it is good to listen to others.

Ways in which adults can value children as individuals	Reasons why this is important for children
Understand what each child enjoys doing and provide activities around these interests.	This will make children feel that they are understood and included. They will feel that their interests are valued.
Allow children to speak and listen to what they say.	This will make children feel that they are important enough to be listened to. This will make them feel respected.
Speak kindly to children.	This will give children the confidence to talk to adults and share their feelings. Children copy the way in which adults speak to others.
Understand that all children have different learning needs.	Meeting children's individual learning needs helps them to develop and learn at their own pace. This will help them to feel valued.
Give all children the support and encouragement they need to play and learn.	This will give children the confidence to try new things and feel proud of themselves.

Table 4.1 How and why adults should value children

CACHE Level 1 Caring for Children

Ways in which adults can value children as individuals	Reasons why this is important for children
Be good role models by learning about different **cultures**.	The adult can encourage children to take an interest in cultures and lifestyles that are different from their own. This will make all children feel valued.
Respect children's different cultures and lifestyles.	This will make children feel that their culture and lifestyle are important.

Table 4.1 How and why adults should value children *(Continued)*

Assessment task 1

1   Draw a spider diagram to show all the ways in which adults can value children as individuals, using Table 4.1 to help you.
2   Think about a young child who attends nursery or school. Think about their **personality** and their likes and needs. Why is it important for adults to respect this child as an individual?

Important words

Culture – the way someone lives, including the ideas, customs and behaviour they have within a society.

Personality – how a person thinks and behaves.

LO2 How to make children feel respected and valued

The way in which an adult behaves towards a child is very important. Children learn from the people around them. If a child grows up seeing the people around them being kind and caring towards others, the child will learn that this is the right way to behave towards other people. If we are kind to them, they will understand that they are important and valued. If a child sees people around them being unkind and bullying, the child will think this type of behaviour is acceptable, when it is not. One way to show children that we respect and value them is through communication.

2.1 Communicating with children to ensure that they feel valued

Communication can be **verbal** and **non-verbal**. Verbal communication is when people use sounds, words and sentences to talk to each other. Non-verbal communication refers to other ways of communicating, such as eye contact, **facial expressions** and body language. (Note that eye contact is not always an appropriate form of communication within some cultures.)

Important words

Facial expressions – these are the ways our faces change (or the look on our faces change), which others use to understand what we mean.

It is very important that adults communicate with children in ways that help them to feel valued and respected. Some ways to communicate well with children include the following suggestions:

◆ **Smile when meeting the child** – this will show that you are pleased to see them.
◆ **Make good eye contact if appropriate** when the child is speaking – this will show that you are interested and are listening to them.
◆ **Stand near to the child, but not too close** – this will respect their need for space.
◆ **Get down to the child's level** – this will make the child feel comfortable and show them that you care enough about what they have to say.
◆ **Use positive language**, such as 'well done' or 'tell me about your picture' – this will show the child that you are interested, and they will feel valued.
◆ **Always listen carefully** to what the child is telling you – this will help the child to feel that you respect what they have to say.
◆ **Take time to answer the child's questions** – this will show the child that you have time for them and are interested in how they feel.

Figure 4.2 It is important to engage with children

2.2 Appropriate adult behaviour towards children

It is important that adults know how to behave in front of children, because children learn by copying what they see and hear. If children see adults treating others with respect, they will learn that this is the right way to behave. It is therefore important that adults are polite, friendly and show children respect, as this will help to make the children feel secure and valued. It is also very important that all adults encourage children to respect each other.

Task

Think about how people treat you in school, college, in the supermarket or in your neighbourhood.
◆ How do they behave towards you?
◆ How does this make you feel?
◆ How do you behave towards them?
◆ How could you behave in a more positive way?

Adults should support the child to understand that everyone is an individual. This includes neighbours, friends, shopkeepers and teachers at school. Differences between children should be seen as positive things that make each child special. If children know that it is a good thing to be different, they may feel good about themselves and respect differences in others.

Other ways to show children that they are valued and respected are shown in Figure 4.3.

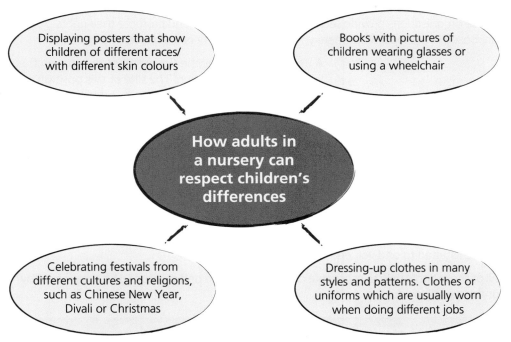

Figure 4.3 How adults in a nursery can respect children's differences

Assessment task 2

1 Write down three ways to communicate with children and say why these ways will make them feel valued (use the list on the previous page (page 34) to help you).

2 Write down three ways of behaving towards children to show that you respect and value them (look at some of the examples in Figure 4.3 to help you).

LO3 Children have rights

3.1 Laws and organisations which support children's rights

Decisions about how a country is run are usually made by the Government. Members of the Government make rules which everyone should follow, called laws. Many laws support children's rights and there are many organisations who care about the lives of children. These organisations provide services to support children and promote their rights. Some are based in the local area where you live, whereas others are based in larger cities.

Task

In pairs, list some of the rights that you think all children should have.

A person is chosen by the Government to focus on the lives and rights of children. The title of this position is 'Minister for Children'. This minister understands that children are important and that they have rights, just like adults.

What are the rights of the child?

Adults who work with children should understand 'The Rights of the Child', which the United Nations Convention on the Rights of the Child promotes for all children in the world. These include the right to:
- feel happy and secure
- be protected from harm
- be listened to and valued
- a health service (doctors, hospitals)
- an education.

All of these rights help to make sure children are valued and grow up to be happy, healthy and responsible adults.

Assessment task 3

Look on the internet or in books to find out about the organisations and people that support the rights of the child.

Summary

In this unit you have learnt that:
- all children must be respected and valued as individuals by the adults around them
- there are many ways to communicate with children to make sure they feel valued and respected
- adults should behave in ways that show children respect
- laws are made to make sure that the rights of children are understood by adults
- there are many organisations that support the rights of the child.

What you will learn in this unit

You will gain an understanding of:

◆ play and leisure activities for children in the community
◆ ways in which children's development can be supported through play and leisure activities
◆ the role of the adult in supporting all children during play and leisure activities.

What are play and leisure?

All children have an equal right to relax and play safely, both on their own and in groups. Children should have the chance to take part in activities that will interest them and help to keep them fit and healthy.

Play is something that interests all children and it is important for their development. It is important that the Government has made laws to try to make sure that all children have the chance to play safely in their community.

Example!

There are centres which provide children with activities after school and during the school holidays. These activity sessions enable children to play safely while their parents may be at work.

Task

Write down a list of places where you can enjoy indoor or outdoor activities in your local area.

LO1 Play and leisure activities for children in the local community

> **!**
>
> ## Important words
>
> **Leisure activities** – activities or hobbies that people might enjoy.
>
> **Local community** – the places and people near to where we live.

1.1, 1.2 Organisations and examples of play and leisure activities available

There are many different kinds of organisations which provide different play and **leisure activities** within a **local community**.

The local council

Local councils provide many different activities for children within the local community. These might include activities in leisure or sports centres, swimming pools, playgrounds and parks. Schools and Early Years Centres often provide after-school clubs and holiday activity sessions.

Voluntary groups

Voluntary groups are usually organised by people who meet to help and support each other and their families. An example of a support group is a group of parents or carers of children with particular needs or a disability, meeting to share experiences and to give their children opportunities to play together. Another example is a group of parents or primary carers running a toddler group together.

Figure 5.1 Swimming is a popular leisure activity and sport

Figure 5.2 Children enjoy belonging to different groups

Voluntary groups include Brownie and Cub/Scout groups that children can join and enjoy activities, learn new skills and sometimes take part in camps and adventure holidays.

Private play companies

Many private companies provide play opportunities for children, such as indoor soft-play centres or 'jungle'-style gyms that enable children to climb, jump and play together on the ropes, slides and in the ball-pool.

Specialist teachers

Specialist teachers give children private lessons in activities, such as music or dance. A specialist teacher could also be a sports coach who gives private football or rugby lessons.

Local sports clubs

Sports clubs often run children's team games or practice sessions, for example, the local cricket club, rugby club or football club.

Figure 5.3 Belonging to a sports club can boost a child's fitness levels and social skills

Churches and religious groups

Religious groups that have indoor halls, such as at a church, and outdoor gardens sometimes allow families and children to use their facilities. Playgroups may be run in the halls and summer fairs may be held in the gardens.

> **Important words**
>
> **Leisure facilities** – places which provide an opportunity to relax and enjoy activities.

Assessment task 1

1 Produce a poster to show local play and **leisure facilities** for children.
2 List four organisations that provide play activities for children and give examples of what these activities could be.

You can use both indoor and outdoor activities for your examples.

LO2 The benefits of play activities for children

2.1 Ways that children's development is supported by play

Children can benefit in many ways from taking part in leisure and play activities. It can support physical development by giving children the opportunity to try new activities, such as basketball or nature walks to enable children to find out about the world around them. Social and emotional development can be improved by taking part in teams or groups, such as football or craft classes. Language and communication skills may also be improved by introducing new words, for example, having to talk about the rules of a game with the team.

Task

In pairs, discuss indoor or outdoor activities that you took part in when you were growing up. How did these activities support your physical development? Did you learn any new words? Which social skills did you need to use?

An example of these benefits can be seen in Table 5.1 on the next page (page 41).

Activity	Area of development	How children's development is being supported
Playing football at the local club	Physical	Running in straight lines and changing direction. Kicking and throwing the ball.
	Social and emotional	Team building, agreeing rules and learning to stay positive when the other team scores. Celebrating together when your team wins.
	Language and communication	Players instructing or telling each other to pass the ball. Learning new words for the different team positions.

Table 5.1 How different activities support children's learning

Assessment task 2

Produce a table like the one above, showing the benefits of taking part in three indoor or outdoor activities.

LO3 The role of adults in supporting play and leisure activities in the community

3.1 How to support children in play and leisure activities

Children need adults to support them, in order to enjoy play and leisure activities. Adults can do this by getting involved in activities in the community, such as volunteering to help at school clubs or sports teams.

The role of the adult is to:
◆ make sure that all children can take part in activities suitable for their age and stage of development
◆ ensure that all the children are included and enjoying the activity
◆ support the children to understand the rules of behaviour and/or the rules of the game
◆ support the children to enjoy team games by organising them into teams or giving roles and responsibilities, such as deciding with the children which child will be goalkeeper first

- supervise all the children to make sure they are playing safely. The adult may need to check the activity for risks and hazards before the children take part – this is called **risk assessment**
- make sure that the equipment and resources are safe for everyone to use.

Figure 5.4 Some adult supervision is required for play and leisure activities

3.2 Factors which might prevent (stop) children from taking part in leisure activities

There are sometimes reasons why families and their children find it difficult to take part in play and leisure activities in their community. For example:

- **lack of clubs or leisure centres –** there may not be any suitable clubs or activities in the local area
- **money** – the activities or equipment may be too expensive for some families, especially if they have quite a large family
- **distance** – a family might live in a rural area and find it difficult to travel to community centres in the local town

> **! Important words**
>
> **Factors preventing children from taking part in leisure activities** – things that stop children from taking part.

- **time of day** – some play and leisure activities may be early in the morning or in the afternoon when families are preparing or having a meal
- **the ages of the children in a family** – parents or carers may have very small children or babies and will need space and activities for them to use as well as the older children
- **parents' and carers' time** – many parents have to work, so may not be able to take their children to the places where play and leisure activities are held. This could also be a problem if the children always need parental supervision
- **illness or disability of a parent or carer** – if a parent has an illness or disability, they may not be able to take their child to different play and leisure activities.

3.3 Including children in play and leisure activities

It is important that adults make sure that all children are included in play and leisure activities. Some children might feel excited about joining in a new activity, but other children may feel anxious when they have to try something new. This anxiety is normal, and all the child may need is some extra time and encouragement from an adult to feel safe and confident enough to take part. Children need to feel that it is okay to not be very good at something, but still enjoy the activity.

Figure 5.5 Children with disabilities should be included in play and leisure activities

For example, most girls and boys who enjoy playing football will never play for a league team, but they may really enjoy taking part in local football matches or just going along to a local park to play with friends. Extra thought and care might be needed if a child has a different need or a disability, for instance appropriate activities and access equipment.

Table 5.2 gives examples of some different needs and disabilities, and ways in which adults can include children.

Particular need or disability	How adults can give support
Asthma: a child may need to be given rest and medication	Supervise the child to make sure that they are given a chair in which to rest. Read medication instructions and make sure medication is given by the responsible adult at the correct time.
Different language: some children may not speak or understand the language	Make sure that the child can join in activities by demonstrating how they are done. Find somebody who speaks the same language so that they can explain or use a translator.
Age of child: a young child may be just beginning to use the potty or toilet	Ask the child if they need the toilet and make sure that they and their parents know where to find the nearest toilet.
A child may not see as well as other children, and may need to wear glasses	Make sure that the child has clean glasses to see through and that the glasses do not become damaged during an activity.
A child may not hear as well as other children, and may need to wear a hearing aid	Make sure that the child can hear and understand any instructions that are being given; speak slowly and clearly.
A child may use a wheelchair	Activities or equipment may need to be changed slightly so that the child can join in, such as the height of tables, ramps into the building or toilets. Adults may need to give one-to-one support to join in certain activities, such as ball games.

Table 5.2 How adults can support children with different needs or disabilities

It is very important that all children are given the opportunity to take part in play and leisure activities in their local community.

Adults need to think about ways of supporting children so that they can take part, which could include finding out about bus routes or organising care for other children in the family. Remember that children with different needs or disabilities may need some special equipment or different support from adults to help them to take part in an activity.

Assessment task 3

1 Choose one of the following leisure activities:
   ◆ a swimming session for children of all ages, in the local swimming pool on Saturday mornings from 9 to 10 am: cost £3.50
   ◆ a dance class in the town hall, from 4.30 to 5.30 pm every Friday, for children aged four to eight years: cost £5.00.
2 Write down two factors which may stop a child from taking part in the chosen activity.
3 Write down ways in which adults can support all children to take part in this activity, including children with different needs or disabilities. Use Table 5.2 to help you.
4 Write down two ways in which the swimming coach or dance teacher will support the children during this session.

Summary

In this unit you have learnt that:

◆ different local organisations provide play and leisure activities for children
◆ children can enjoy many different indoor and outdoor activities in their local community
◆ children's physical, social and emotional development, and language and communication skills can be supported through taking part in play and leisure activities
◆ some children may need extra support from adults to help them take part in play and leisure activities.

Chapter 6
CFC 16 Preparing for your next steps

What you will learn in this unit

You will gain an understanding of:

◆ how to achieve your chosen career
◆ how to find out about training courses and jobs
◆ how you should describe your skills and experience in a CV
◆ how to apply for jobs and prepare for an interview.

LO1 Personal career goals

1.1 Investigate career goals

It is important that when you are making decisions about a future **career**, you have plenty of information and advice to help you make choices. There are many different **jobs** in the childcare world, and many different childcare courses that give you the qualifications you need to work with children. It is important that you understand the skills you need to do the job, for example, when working with children or older adults you need to be able to follow rules and instructions to keep everyone safe. It is also important that you know the personal qualities that are needed. For example, when working with children you need to be a good role model and be calm and kind.

Important words

Career goals – what you want to achieve from your career.

Career – a job that you do for a long or extended period of time, and can take you in a certain direction, for example, childcare or nursing.

Job – work that you do in order to earn money.

1.2 Next steps

It is important to spend time thinking about what career goals you would like to achieve. When you have found a job or career that you are interested in, you need to look at the next steps to take in order to make this happen.

There are usually a number of steps that need to be taken to reach a goal. Figure 6.1 shows examples of the different steps to be taken by a person who wants to work with children.

It may be helpful to think about **training** courses or experience that you will need to gain a job in this area of interest. Figure 6.2 on the next page (page 48) gives examples of the kinds of training, skills and job opportunities that are available in this area.

Important words

Training – courses which help a person to gain skills or qualifications.

Task

Use the internet to find out about the different courses you could take or the childcare jobs you could apply for.

You could also think about the personal qualities you may need to do the job well.

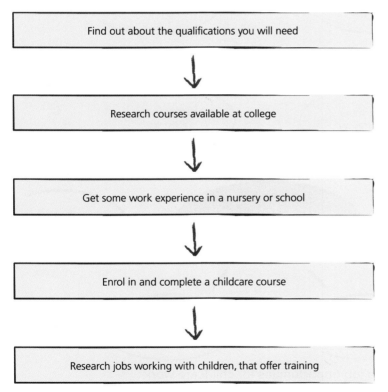

Find out about the qualifications you will need

↓

Research courses available at college

↓

Get some work experience in a nursery or school

↓

Enrol in and complete a childcare course

↓

Research jobs working with children, that offer training

Figure 6.1 Examples of steps leading to a career in childcare

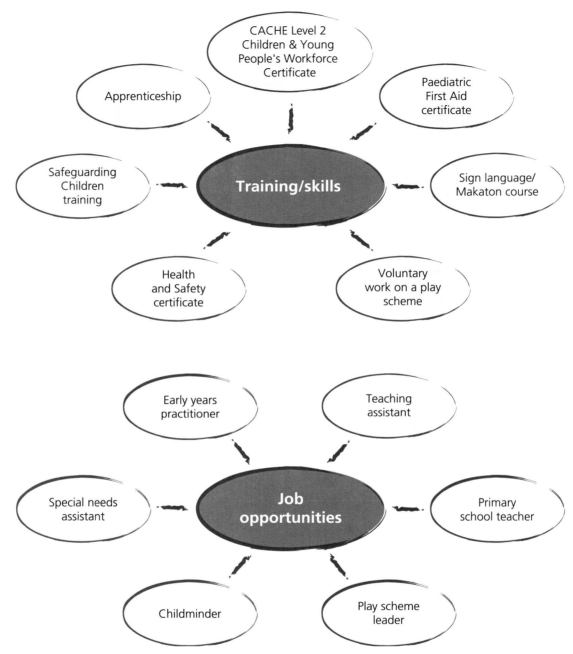

Figure 6.2 Training, skills and job opportunities for childcare work

1.3 Possible barriers to reaching career goals

There may be reasons which make it more difficult for the next steps to be taken, when you are trying to reach your career goals. These are known as '**barriers**' and it is important to think about how you can get around them, so that they do not stop you from taking further steps on the path to your chosen career.

Figure 6.4 gives examples of possible barriers to reaching your career goals.

> **Important words**
>
> **Barriers** – things that may get in the way of achievement.

Figure 6.3 There are many steps to take to have a career in childcare

Figure 6.4 Possible barriers to reaching your career goals

Assessment task 1

Using a table like Table 6.1:
- ◆ write a list of your career goals or jobs that you would like to do
- ◆ write down the next steps that can be taken to reach these goals
- ◆ write down some of the problems or barriers that might stand in your way.

My career goals	What do I need to do next (next steps)?	What might stop me from doing this?

Table 6.1 Considering your career path

LO2 Understand opportunities for training and work

2.1, 2.2, 2.3 Sources of information about training and employment

You can find information about training courses and job vacancies in a chosen career in many places.

Example!
- ◆ The internet
- ◆ Newspapers
- ◆ The job centre
- ◆ Popular childcare magazines
- ◆ College information booklets
- ◆ A careers advisor

Assessment task 2

In pairs:
- ◆ find information about training or jobs with children that you are interested in
- ◆ using this information, decide which steps you would need to take to get this job or go on this course.

LO3 How to prepare for work or training

3.1 Outlining your personal skills

When you are going along a chosen **career path** and applying for training courses or jobs, it is important to think about your own skills and qualities, your interests and experiences.

> **Important words**
>
> **Career path** – the direction in which a person takes their career.

Task

Copy Figure 6.5 and write down your:
◆ skills (what you can do well, for example, being organised, good timekeeping, good team player, good communication)
◆ qualities (positive things that you can bring to a job, such as being helpful, patient and caring)
◆ interests and work experience.

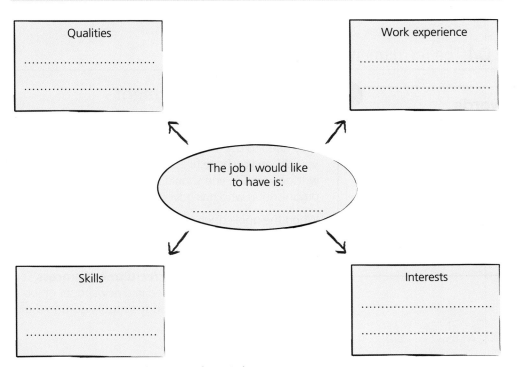

Figure 6.5 Your qualifications for a job

3.2, 3.3 Creating a CV

Often when you apply for a job, you will be asked to provide a Curriculum Vitae or **CV**. This is simply information about yourself that you need to give to the person or company that has advertised the job. They use this information to choose the person most suitable for the job.

There is an example of a CV in Figure 6.6 on the next page (page 53).

> ## Important words
>
>
>
> **CV** – a list of your skills and knowledge.

> ### Assessment task 3
>
> Use the sample CV in Figure 6.6 to create your own CV. Think about all the information that will be needed: a brief description of your qualifications, skills and experience which would relate to your identified career path. Also take time to include relevant personal information which may help you to get an interview.

Task

Look at the CV in Figure 6.6 in small groups. Do you think this person shows that they have the skills and qualities to work with children?

LO4 The recruitment process

> ## Important words
>
> **Recruitment** – how a person with the right skills can be found and chosen for the right job.
>
> **Recruitment process** – applying for a job, preparing and going for an interview. From the employer's side, this involves advertising the job vacancy, interviewing and hiring the right person.

4.1 Steps to recruitment

Once you have seen a job advertisement that you are interested in, you will need to apply for the job. You may need to ask for an application form to be sent to you. When you have filled out the application form or written your CV, you should send it to the person or organisation who has advertised the job vacancy.

When the application has been looked at, you may be asked to go for an interview if your skills, qualities and experience match the needs of the job.

This process is known as the **recruitment process**. It starts when a job is advertised in a newspaper or job centre and ends with somebody suitable getting the job and starting work.

Corinne Victoria Ward
17 X Street
Wakefield
DX19 9XZ
T: 01999 000000
E: c_v_ward@cachemail.com

I am a hard-working early years student studying on the CACHE level 1 childcare course. I try very hard to gain good grades, and when I finish the course in July 2021, I hope to achieve a good grade. I am organised and always hand my work in on time. I am polite and respectful to others and my college reports say that I am beginning to develop all the skills required to be a good childcare assistant. I am patient, kind and really enjoy looking after young children.

In my spare time, I enjoy jogging and I have recently run in a half marathon. I had to plan my training for this race and train properly to make sure I was fit for the race. I think this shows that when I am focused on doing something, I can be successful. In my spare time I also enjoy babysitting my cousin who is four years old, and I would love to work with children.

Qualifications

Subject	Level	Grade	School/college	Date
Food Hygiene	Certificate	Pass	Food Safety Limited	2019
English Language	GCSE	4	Winterset Common School	2020
Maths	GCSE	3	Winterset Common School	2020
Art	Level 1	Pass	Winterset Common School	2020
First Aid	Certificate	Pass	Central College	2021
CACHE level 1 childcare	Certificate	complete July 2021	Central College	

Work experience/jobs

Place of work	Job title	Responsibilities	Date start–finish
Rob's Fish and Chips Street Side Rd	Catering assistant	Mainly responsible for serving customers and making sure that the serving area is kept clean at all times. After closing time I help to wash all the surfaces and floors.	Jan 19–present

Hobbies and interests
I enjoy keeping fit by swimming and I go for a five-mile run every weekend. I enjoy being with my family and playing with my four-year-old cousin. I often go to the cinema with my friends at the weekend.

References can be gained from

Emma Barker	Robert Fryer
College Tutor	Rob's Fish and Chips
Central College	Street Side Rd

Figure 6.6 A sample CV

Assessment task 4a

It is important to understand the recruitment process so that you know what needs to be done when you are applying for a job.

In pairs, look at the steps below. Put into the correct order the steps you should take to secure a job.

◆ Complete application form and/or write CV
◆ Accept the offer of an interview
◆ Submit application form and/or CV
◆ Accept job offer
◆ Look for suitable job vacancies
◆ Attend interview
◆ Prepare for the interview

Even though you have applied for a job, you may not get it. It is important to stay positive and keep trying, as usually many people apply for the same job.

4.2 Preparing for an interview

The more prepared you are, the more chance you have of being successful. It is very important to prepare well before an interview. See Figure 6.8 on the next page (page 55), which includes some tips on preparing well for an interview.

Assessment task 4b

Write down four reasons to be well prepared for an interview.

Figure 6.7 You will feel much more confident at an interview if you have prepared well

Think about the questions that you could ask at the interview. It is important to ask questions of your own as this shows that you are interested and have taken the time to think about what you will be doing

It is very important to arrive on time to the interview: plan your journey so that you know what transport to take or how long it will take to walk

Make sure you read all of the job information carefully

Good preparation for an interview

Make a note of the skills and experience you have that match the job role

It is important to sleep well the night before so that you look and feel fresh

Think about the questions that you may be asked in the interview, and think about the answers you could give. This will show that you understand what the job requires you to do

Take some time to think about how you should dress. You should be clean and tidy and wear smart clothes. This will show that you are a suitable person for the job

Figure 6.8 Good preparation for an interview

Summary

In this unit you have learnt that:

◆ you need to know which steps to take to reach your career goals

◆ barriers sometimes get in the way of taking next steps

◆ there are many opportunities for training and jobs, and you can find information in many places

◆ it is very important to prepare yourself when applying for jobs and training courses

◆ a CV contains information that could help you to get a job, and it is important to include all your skills and qualities that are needed for the job

◆ it is important to prepare well for an interview to make sure that you have a good chance of being successful.

Chapter 7
CFC 17 Supporting babies to play

> ### What you will learn in this unit
> You will gain an understanding of:
> ◆ ways of supporting babies' development through play
> ◆ the different play activities for babies (from birth to 15 months)
> ◆ the role of the adult when providing play activities for babies.
>
> You will also learn about toys and activities suitable for babies from birth to 15 months.

LO1 Supporting babies' development by play

1.1, 1.2 Supporting babies' development and individual needs through play

Play is sometimes called 'children's work' because it is something that most children and babies like to spend their time doing. When children and babies play, they are having fun and will be learning lots of new things.

Play is a very important way to support babies' individual needs and development because it gives them many opportunities to explore and try new things. Babies will spend time exploring objects with their senses, for example, picking up a rattle with their hands and putting it near their mouths to feel the texture and shape. They need to be given lots of different objects to explore so that they can begin to understand more about the world around them.

> **Important words**
>
> **Physical development** – when our bodies grow and we gain new skills, for example, jumping and riding a bike.

Babies' **physical development** is supported through play as they start to move their bodies. To begin with they may only grasp a toy with their hands, but as they grow and develop babies will crawl around and use more muscles. Play helps them to develop strong muscles and a sense of balance when they move, as well as good hand–eye co-ordination when they pick up and move toys.

Because a young baby is not able to move to explore what is around them, they need children and adults to help them. By giving the baby toys to explore or by showing them new things, they will soon begin to understand more about the world around them, how things work and what things do. This understanding is known as the baby's **intellectual development**. For example, the baby will learn that if they drop a ball it will fall and roll away, but if they drop a teddy it falls but does not roll away. The teddy will not make much sound if it is dropped, but a cup will make a loud noise.

Language development is supported through play because when adults spend time playing with children, they usually talk about what they are doing. This often happens without the adult having to think about what they are saying. For example, if you give a baby a toy dog, the adult will usually say something like 'look, it's a brown dog,' or if the baby drops a spoon the adult might say 'oh look, you've dropped your spoon!' This conversation will help the baby to start to understand what different words and phrases mean.

Important words

Intellectual development – when our brain develops and we begin to understand more, for example, children learn to read and write.

Language development – this starts when a baby is born and begins to communicate by crying. The baby hears sounds and begins to copy what they have heard. This is the beginning of language development.

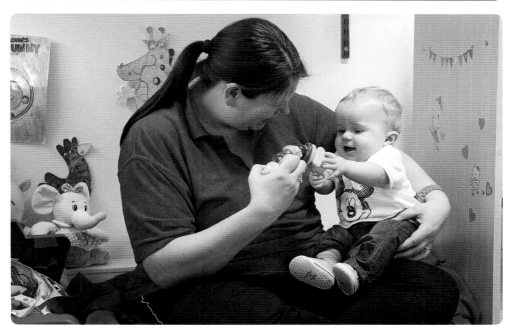

Figure 7.1 A baby's development should be supported through play

Babies can practise holding and moving toys. For example, a baby shaking a rattle will learn about how to make sounds by holding and moving an object. A baby may learn the names and sounds of farm animals when playing with a toy farm.

Figures 7.2, 7.3 and 7.4 show ways in which to support babies' physical development, intellectual and language development, and social and emotional development.

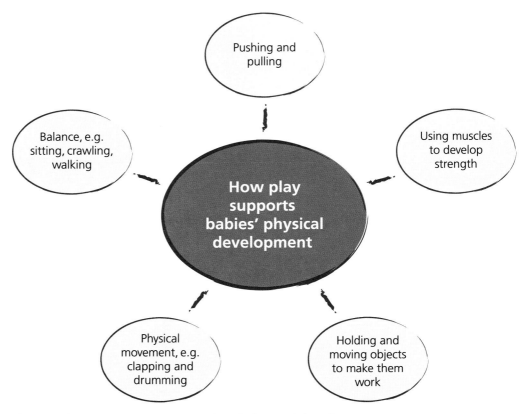

Figure 7.2 How play supports babies' physical development

Figure 7.3 How play supports babies' intellectual and language development

Important words

Emotional development – the development of many different feelings, from sad to happy and excited to angry.

Social development – understanding the needs of others as well as your own and understanding how to behave in different places.

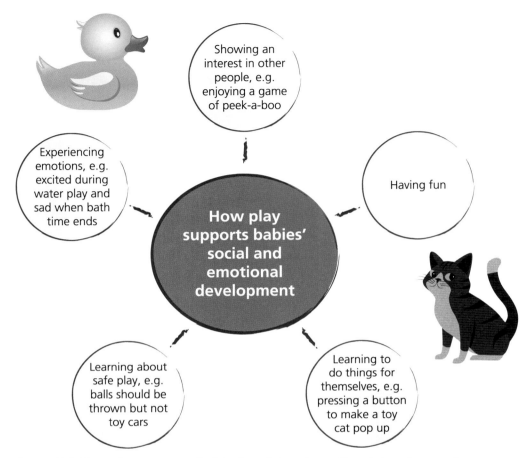

Figure 7.4 How play supports babies' social and emotional development

CACHE Level 1 Caring for Children

LO2 Play activities for babies

2.1, 2.2 Play activities, resources and benefits for babies (from birth to 15 months)

> **Important words**
>
> **Resources** – toys and equipment.

Age of child	Activity	Resources	Benefits for the baby
Birth to three months	Listening to music	Musical toys	Music can soothe a crying baby.
	Watching moving objects	Mobiles	Babies will enjoy trying to focus their eyes on the hanging toy.
Three to seven months	Exploring, kicking and rolling	Musical animal play mat	Physical movement to reach and touch the animals; hearing the sounds the animals make.
	Bath-time play	Floating fish	Grasping the fish in the water helps to develop physical skills.
Seven to 12 months	Building towers and knocking them over	Soft cubes	Learning how to build a tower and enjoying watching it fall over.
	Hand painting	Paints and paper	Enjoy feeling the textures and looking at the patterns in the paint.
12–15 months	First steps	Push-along trolley	Helps with balance and physical strength and development.
	Story time	Glove puppets	Encourages young children to talk and concentrate on the puppet.

Table 7.1 Benefits of different toys and **resources** for a baby

3.1 Ensuring babies can play safely

It is the job (role) of the adult to choose toys that are suitable and safe for the age of the baby. If babies are given toys that are too difficult for them to use, they will not enjoy playing with them and they could harm the baby.

Toy safety

Some toys may have very small parts which makes them unsafe for babies and young children. Adults must ensure that the toys which babies and young children play with are safe. All toys sold in the UK should display a symbol which shows the safety and quality of the toy. Table 7.2 shows the different safety symbols used on toys, games and clothes.

Safety symbol	What does it mean?
0-3 logo	This logo means that the toy is not suitable for children under the age of three years. The under-threes put everything into their mouths to explore shape and texture. If they are given toys which have small parts, younger children could swallow or choke on them. Toys with this sign should not be given to children under three years.
Lion Mark	The Lion Mark was developed by the British Toy and Hobby Association (BTHA), which supply around 90 per cent of toys sold in the UK. It was created in 1988 as a symbol of safety and quality.
CE	The CE mark on a toy label means that the toy meets all the safety standards required by current European law.
BEAB Approved	The BEAB Approved mark is an electrical safety mark found on electrical items used in the home, including children's equipment. This symbol means that the equipment has been made correctly and is safe to use.

Table 7.2 Safety symbols found on children's equipment, clothing and toys

Age-appropriate toys

Some companies that sell toys write messages on the packaging to help you choose a suitable toy. For example, it might state 'recommended for children aged three to four years.'

Age guidelines can help you choose the right toy for the baby or young child. For example, a ten-piece jigsaw is too difficult for babies aged 11 months, so they would not enjoy or learn from this activity.

Task

Using a catalogue or pictures from the internet, make a collage showing a collection of toys suitable for these age groups:
◆ birth to six months
◆ six to 12 months
◆ 12–18 months.

Remember the safety marks! A toy that is not suitable for children under the age of three years should not be chosen for these age groups.

3.2 How adults can encourage babies to play

Babies and young children are individuals; they learn in different ways and are interested in different things. When providing toys and activities for babies, adults should think about their ages and interests. By choosing toys and equipment which are suitable for the baby's age and ability, you are supporting the baby to have fun and learn through play.

Toys do not have to be expensive or have a purpose. For example, when given a present, some babies will show more interest in exploring the packaging or the box than in the present inside. They may have fun pulling the packaging apart or listening to the crunchy sound of wrapping paper. This means babies can be given lots of inexpensive/cheap items and materials to support their development, such as cardboard boxes, washed plastic containers or pots and pans to play with.

Task

Plan a treasure basket for a baby aged 6–8 months. What items and materials would you include to support their development?

What words or phrases would you use to support the baby's language development?

Below are some guidelines for providing and supporting play activities.

◆ Provide suitable clothing for messy play.
◆ Check that equipment such as paintbrushes and crayons are suitable for the baby's age.
◆ Provide toys and materials which could help the baby to learn new skills.
◆ Make sure that the play area is safe and there are no dangers, for example, cables and plug sockets.
◆ Check that there is enough space for the baby to be able to move around safely.
◆ Observe the baby to make sure that they are safe and enjoying the activity.
◆ Show the baby that you are interested by smiling and using supportive language, for example, 'you do it', 'clever boy'.
◆ Support the baby to explore the toy to find out how it works or what it does.
◆ Remember that the baby needs time to find things out for themselves – do not take over the baby's play.
◆ Support the baby when they need it, for example, show the baby how the toy works if they are struggling.
◆ Make sure that the area is inviting by using bright toys and perhaps soft music.

Figure 7.5 An adult can support a baby's development through play

Task

In pairs, choose three toys for babies aged birth to 15 months. State what age each toy is suitable for and why the toys could be good to support a baby's development.

Copy Table 7.3, which explores the role of the adult in supporting babies' development and needs through different activities. Fill in the blank cells with your own examples.

Age of child	Activity, toy or resources that might be used	Area of development being supported	Role of the adult in supporting individual needs
Birth to three months	Hanging a musical toy on the baby's pram		Choosing toys that are suitable by checking the safety symbols and recommended age. Always watching to make sure that the baby is safe. Removing the toy when the baby has had enough or is too tired.
Three to seven months	Placing the baby onto a colourful play mat		Always watching to make sure that the baby is safe. Making sure that there are no dangers around the mat, such as plug sockets or toys that the child could roll onto. Understanding when the child has had enough.
Seven to 12 months		Social and emotional development	
12–15 months	Making pictures using different colour play foam on paper. Resources: ◆ foam (different colours) ◆ plastic bowls ◆ large sheets of paper		

Table 7.3 How activities and adults can support learning through play

Assessment task 2

Design a poster to show what adults need to do to keep babies safe during play.

On the poster, include five ways that adults can encourage babies to play.

Summary

In this unit you have learnt that:
◆ play is good for babies' development
◆ safety is very important when babies are enjoying play.

Chapter 8

CFC 21 Science activities for young children

LO1 Science activities suitable for young children

Children of all ages enjoy experimenting and investigating the world around them. They like to find out about how things work and what they do.

Children use their senses to discover new things: see Figure 8.1 on the next page (page 67).

Example!

By using all their senses, children have the opportunity to find out about the world around them.

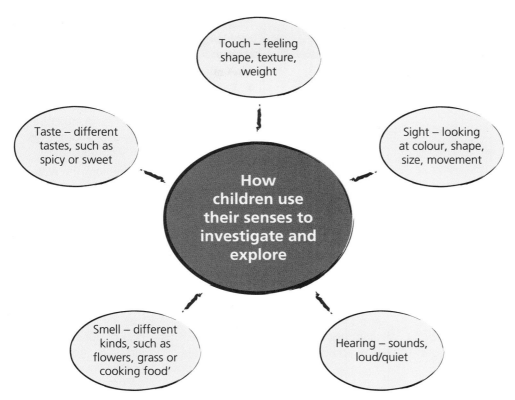

Figure 8.1 Using senses to explore the world

Often adults do not pay attention to things that happen around them in everyday life; they are so used to seeing them that they do not think about them. However, often these will be new experiences for children.

1.1 Science activities for different ages

Age of child	Science activity	Description of the activity	Resources needed	Health and safety
18 months to two years	Wet sand play	Adding water gradually to a sand tray, so that children can feel how the texture of the sand changes as the water is added.	◆ Sand tray ◆ Sand ◆ Plastic jug ◆ Water ◆ Aprons (to keep child dry)	Spilled water should be mopped up so that no one slips. Children should be supervised closely so that they do not throw sand or put it in their mouths.

Table 8.1 Some suitable science activities to do with children

Age of child	Science activity	Description of the activity	Resources needed	Health and safety
18 months to two years	Ice cube water play	Put ice cubes into a bowl of warm water and enable the children to feel the ice melting and watch the cubes become smaller and disappear as they melt.	◆ Plastic bowl ◆ Warm water ◆ Ice cubes (frozen in advance) ◆ Aprons	Mop up water spills. Supervise children to make sure they do not put ice cubes into their mouths (as they could choke). Make sure the water is only warm and not too hot.
18 months to two years	Washing dolls' clothes and hanging them up to dry			
Three to five years	Planting a sunflower seed and watching it grow	Children plant a seed in a plastic plant pot filled with compost. Children water the seed regularly. Children will see the plant begin to grow and see the leaves and petals open.	◆ Plastic plant pot and saucer (stops the water leaking onto the floor) ◆ Sunflower seeds ◆ Compost ◆ Small watering can	Supervise children to make sure that they do not put seeds into their mouths, and to ensure they do not eat or throw compost. Mop up water spills. Wash hands after touching compost.

Table 8.1 Some suitable science activities to do with children *(Continued.*
Note that some columns are intentionally left blank as you will be required
to fill them in as part of the Assessment task on page 70.*)*

Age of child	Science activity	Description of the activity	Resources needed	Health and safety
Three to five years	Making chocolate crispy cakes	Melt chocolate in a bowl over a pan of hot water. Add cornflakes or crispies and stir well until the chocolate covers all the cornflakes. Put cupcake cases into a cupcake baking tray. Spoon the mixture into the cases and allow them to cool in the fridge.	◆ Pan of hot water ◆ Bowl ◆ Wooden spoon ◆ Chocolate bars ◆ Cornflakes or crispies ◆ Aprons ◆ Cupcake cases ◆ Cupcake baking tray ◆ Fridge	Make sure that everyone washes their hands before starting the activity. Make sure children do not burn themselves on the pan of hot water: explain the dangers to the children. Remove the pan from the children once the chocolate has melted. Do not leave the children alone with the hot water. Mop up water spills.
Three to five years	Finding out about floating and sinking in a water tray			

Table 8.1 Some suitable science activities to do with children *(Continued.* Note that some columns are intentionally left blank as you will be required to fill them in as part of the Assessment task on page 70.)

Example!

Examples of other science activities you could do with children include:

◆ watching cakes rising in the oven
◆ seeing how boiling water makes steam
◆ watching spring flowers pushing up through the earth
◆ hearing the leaves crunch under their feet in autumn
◆ feeling ice cream melting in their hands on a hot day
◆ touching wet clothes as they dry on the line
◆ tasting new foods and experiencing how they feel on the tongue.

LO2 Setting up science activities to support young children's learning

Task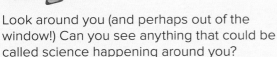

Look around you (and perhaps out of the window!) Can you see anything that could be called science happening around you?

Important words

Resources – the equipment and tools needed for an activity.

Health and safety risks – things or situations that could be dangerous and cause harm.

Figure 8.2 Children can enjoy learning about science through play

2.1, 2.2 Resources and possible health and safety risks for science activities

Resources

These are the equipment or tools that will be needed for the activity. You will need to prepare these before the activity begins.

Health and safety

When planning science activities for children, it is always important to think about everyone's health and safety.

Example!

If you are baking with children and using the oven or a hot surface, it is important to keep children safe and explain the dangers to them. Sharp equipment should always be kept out of the reach of young children.

Assessment task 1

Look back at the science activities in Table 8.1. Copy and complete the table to show how you would prepare a washing-and-drying activity for children aged 18 months to two years, and a floating and sinking activity for children aged three to five years.

2.3 Supporting children who are carrying out science activities

Science activities support children's understanding of the world around them and of how things work and what things do. For example, children playing with cars on a mat will be discovering about pushing and pulling and how things move.

Adults need to understand that sometimes children need space and time to find out things for themselves. If the child playing with the cars on a mat is enjoying moving the cars around, an adult should watch and not interrupt. However, if the child becomes bored, the adult could give the child a ramp to see if the car moves faster.

At other times the child may need support to carry out the activity. This could be because it involves a danger, such as heat, or it could be because the child does not really understand how to do something, such as how to make cakes or buns.

Adults should:
◆ support children by making sure that they have the correct resources available to carry out the science activity
◆ always think about health and safety and keep children safe while doing the activity
◆ think about ways to support children to learn new things while enjoying the activity.

Figure 8.3 Children need careful supervision for some science activities

Look back at the science activities you have completed in Assessment task 1.
1 Draw a spider diagram to show what the children could learn from each activity.
2 Write down what kind of support the children may need from adults during each activity. (Remember that this will include resources, health and safety and supporting the children to understand.)

LO3 What young children can gain from doing science activities

3.1 Expected learning from each activity

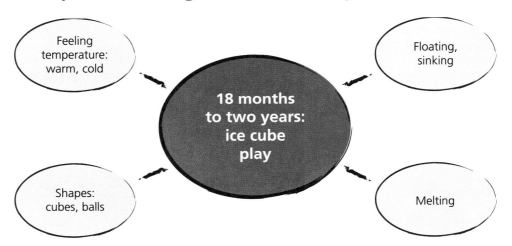

Figure 8.4 Examples of what young children can learn from doing science activities

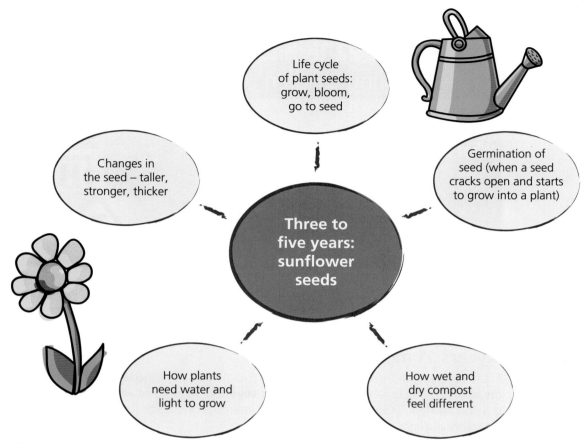

Figure 8.4 Examples of what young children can learn from doing science activities *(Continued)*

Summary

In this unit you have learnt that:

◆ many science activities are suitable for young children
◆ adults need to think carefully about setting up science activities and the resources that may be needed
◆ adults should always make sure that children are safe by thinking about their health and safety
◆ children will need different types of support to enjoy the activities
◆ young children can learn many new things from science activities when adults support their learning.

> ### What you will learn in this unit
> You will gain an understanding of:
> - technology toys and activities that are suitable for young children
> - how technology toys and activities can help to support children's learning and development.

LO1 Technology toys or activities suitable for children

1.1 Technology toys or activities for children up to 5 years 11 months

There are many different **technology toys** available to buy for children. Toy designers are always trying to design new **electronic toys** and games that will help children to develop and learn. Children are usually very interested in toys that make sounds or have flashing lights or colourful pictures.

Children will often play with an electronic toy for longer than a doll or a car, for example, as the electronic toy may change what it sounds like or what it does. A game on a tablet, for example, will give the child more of a challenge and as the child gets better at the game, they may play on the tablet for longer. It may give the child praise, such as saying 'well done' or by playing a sound when the child does something correctly, or it may say 'try again' if the child has not yet managed a task. This feedback keeps the child interested and makes them feel like they are doing well.

> ### Important words
>
> **Technology toys** – toys which usually have some kind of simple built-in computer.
>
> **Electronic toys** – toys and games that need power to work, usually from electricity or batteries.

Until recently, many electronic toys and games that were designed for children had to be used when the child was sitting down or being still. This meant that some children were not getting much exercise when they were playing with the toys, which was seen as a bad thing. Technology toys are now being designed so that children need to move around to use them, for example, sports games on a games console may need children to move around and use their muscles to play the game well.

Figure 9.1 Some technology toys can be used from birth

Babies from birth to one year

A range of technology toys are available for babies, such as electronic books, soft animals that make sounds and electronic activity mats. Popular technology toys for babies include educational activities on bouncers and baby gyms where babies can touch buttons to activate lights and sounds. There is a wide range of tablet and smartphone apps that are designed for babies. These usually have simple pictures and sounds to keep the baby interested or have music and moving pictures that attract the baby's attention.

To help support the baby's development, it is important for adults to share this technology play with the baby, to encourage them to learn and to develop the baby's communication and social skills. For example, the baby may be enjoying listening to a nursery rhyme on a tablet, but if the adult claps and joins in with the song it will encourage the baby to join in too.

Toddlers aged one to two years

When children reach the toddler stage, there are many different technology toys and activities that they can enjoy.

Apps and games on tablets and smartphones are designed to meet the needs of very young children and can be a great way to help children to learn. For example, children can learn the names of animals and the noises they make or learn about colours, but adults will need to help and encourage children to play and use the technology. For example, adults will need to turn on the device and find the app or game for the child to enjoy.

Example!

◆ Pretend phones that make sounds
◆ Story readers
◆ Play computers that help children to learn the names of objects, numbers or colours
◆ Electronic dolls that make sounds
◆ Push-along walker toys

Children aged three to five years

There are even more educational technology toys and activities for this age range. Computer programs and apps for tablets and smartphones can teach children shapes, numbers, letters and sounds. Child-friendly digital cameras are popular for this age group.

There are computer games and apps which can give children the chance to be active while they are learning, for example, music and dance games. It is important that adults support children when they are playing and learning from this technology because children's speaking, listening and social skills are just as important as learning new things on their own.

Task

Look at the activity centre in Figure 9.2. When a child presses each button, the name of the picture is sounded.
- Think of a topic that young children might be interested in.
- Design your own activity centre, adding picture buttons for children to press. Write down what the buttons will do.
- Think of other actions or features that could be added to your activity centre, such as flashing lights or music.

Figure 9.2 An activity centre

LO2 How technology toys and activities support learning and development

1.2, 2.1 Benefits for the child of using technology toys

There are many benefits for children of using technology toys:

◆ Children can learn the rules of an activity and how to take turns, for example, a bowling game on a games console teaches children to take turns, to count and to develop control of the hand-held remote control.

◆ Children learn that it is alright for them to make mistakes and that if they try again, they will get better at the activity with practice.

◆ Benefits to physical development could include helping a child to learn how to control their bodies or improve their balance.

◆ Benefits to intellectual and language development could include learning the names of colours, learning how to count, and learning new words or how to copy sounds.

Figure 9.3 Using digital cameras can be fun for young children

2.2 How technology toys can support children's development

As we have seen in this chapter so far, technology toys can help children to learn many things and can boost their physical, intellectual and language development. Figure 9.4 shows examples of the kinds of things technology toys can support the learning of.

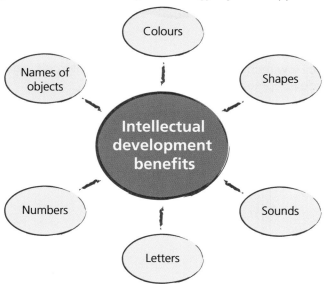

Figure 9.4a How technology toys can support children's learning (intellectual development benefits)

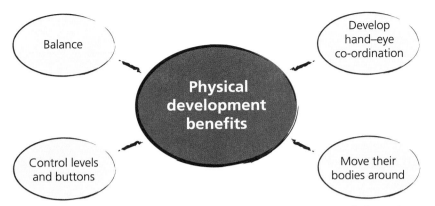

Figure 9.4b How technology toys can support children's learning (physical development benefits)

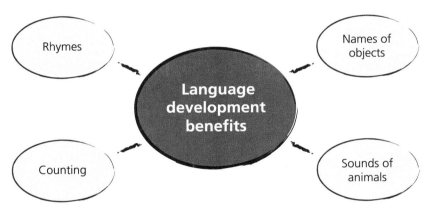

Figure 9.4c How technology toys can support children's learning (language development benefits)

Task

Have a look online or in catalogues at the different technology toys available for children. Write down some of the benefits listed in the information given about the toys.

You could also write down what an adult can do to help the child to learn even more, when playing with each technology toy.

Assessment task

1. Make a poster using pictures of nine technology toys cut out from magazines or catalogues for:
   ◆ three toys for children from birth to 12 months
   ◆ three toys for children aged one to two years
   ◆ three toys for children aged three to five years.
2. Write down the physical, intellectual and language benefits for children when they use the toys you have chosen.

Summary

In this unit you have learnt that:

◆ young children can enjoy many technology toys and activities which can help them to learn while being active

◆ technology toys and activities can support children's physical skills, and their intellectual and language development

◆ adults need to support the child when they are playing with a technology toy to support their learning and development.

Chapter 10

CFC 23 Musical activities for young children

What you will learn in this unit

You will gain an understanding of:

◆ the benefits of musical activities for young children (aged three months to five years)

◆ how to plan musical activities

◆ how to make safe musical instruments for young children

◆ what young children can learn from musical activities.

LO1 Benefits of musical activities for young children

1.1, 1.2 Suitable musical activities and their benefits

Most people enjoy listening to music. Some people enjoy playing **musical instruments** to make their own music, while others prefer to dance or exercise to music. Most people have a favourite type of music, such as classical music, rap or pop. Some people listen to music to relax or to try to change their mood. Others find it easier to concentrate when they are listening to music, such as when doing homework.

Children also enjoy listening to and making sounds. These sounds can be called music if they have some kind of rhythm or beat.

The sounds of the music can make children behave differently, so it is important that adults choose music that is suitable for the time of day. For example, a soft lullaby song will soothe babies and children and can be used to help them to sleep. Music with a strong beat and a lively sound can encourage children to dance and move around, so it would not be sensible to play this type of music just before bedtime.

Important words

Musical instruments – objects that make musical sounds.

Babies might feel soothed by soft music playing and will often show they are enjoying the sounds of the music by stopping crying or turning their heads to show they are listening, or by using their arms and legs to move to the sounds they can hear. Adults can give babies opportunities to enjoy music by singing to them, playing music to them or giving them musical toys, such as jingle bells, musical cot mobiles or soft toys that play a tune.

It is important that the music is not played too loudly as young babies have very **sensitive hearing** that can easily be damaged. Loud noises could also scare young children.

Figure 10.1 Playing with musical instruments is a popular activity for children

Figure 10.2 Babies sometimes find music soothing

Important words

Sensitive hearing – when someone is aware of very small sounds.

Task

Use catalogues and magazines to cut out pictures of musical toys and instruments for babies and young children.
◆ What age of child is each toy or instrument suitable for?
◆ What can children do with each toy or instrument?

Copy and complete Table 10.1 to show what the children could enjoy and learn from each musical activity.

Age of child	Suitable activity or musical toy	What the children could enjoy and learn
Three to 12 months	◆ Cot mobile ◆ Soft musical toy ◆ Soft music played from a CD or download	The child might enjoy listening to the sounds and watching the mobile move. Young children quickly learn that a certain toy makes a sound and will enjoy listening to the sound. You can buy toys with a gentle rhythm that sounds just like a heartbeat, which can help to soothe a distressed baby. Even very young babies might feel comforted and soothed by the sound of soft music being played.
One to two and a half years	◆ Musical activity centre ◆ Drums and pans	
Two and a half to five years	◆ Making a shaker ◆ Singing along to familiar music and songs	

Table 10.1 Musical activities suitable for young children

LO2 Making musical activities and games for young children

2.1, 2.2, 2.3 Musical instruments and games and their value for learning

Children enjoy experimenting with the sounds that different instruments make. They will be excited about making and using their own instruments. Adults need to make sure that the materials they use to make musical instruments with children are suitable and cannot cause any harm. For example, small beads or dried beans make really good sounds when they are put into containers and shaken. However, young children could put these beads in their mouths during the activity, so need to be closely watched by an adult.

Instruments which children can make

There are many different instruments that adults can make with young children. Different materials can make different sounds. Some examples are:

◆ **Sandpaper blocks**: These are two small blocks or bricks which are both covered on one side with coarse sandpaper. The blocks are rubbed together to make a 'rasping' sound.
◆ **Musical triangle**: Wire coat hangers are bent into a triangle shape. The hook of the coat hanger is bent down so that string can be threaded through for the child to hold. A metal spoon can be used to 'ting' on the side of the triangle.
◆ **Ice-cream tub drums**: Empty ice-cream tubs can be decorated and used as drums. Wooden spoons can be used as drumsticks.

Figure 10.3 Plastic bottles can also be used to make instruments

Task

Look at the examples above and then use the internet, books or magazines to find out about other instruments that are suitable to be made by young children.

You could also write down ways the adult could help the children to enjoy playing with these instruments.

Musical activities and games

Children often enjoy activities and games where music is played. Music is frequently used within activities to encourage children to dance or move. Children might enjoy games such as 'musical chairs' or 'musical statues', in which music is played and suddenly turned off; children then have to find and sit on a chair or stand very still.

Some children's television programmes use music or songs to encourage children to sing, copy actions or join in with dance moves.

Assessment task 2

Choose one of the above ideas for making an instrument or think of your own idea and then plan the musical activity. Use the sample activity plan in Table 10.2 to help you.

Activity plan to make a musical shaker	
Age of children and numbers of children	◆ Two to five years. ◆ Children aged two years will do the activity on their own with the adult. Older children will be in groups of three.
Resources	◆ Plastic bottles with tightly fitting lids ◆ Strong sticky tape ◆ Dried beans, small dried pasta shapes, rice or sand (to make sounds in the bottles)
What the children will do	1 Children will carefully wash out the bottles and dry them completely with a cloth or towel. 2 Children will tip a small amount of one of the dry products into the bottle and screw on the lid tightly. 3 The strong sticky tape should be wrapped around the lid to make sure it cannot be taken off.
What the children will learn	◆ Children will enjoy making the shaker. ◆ Children will enjoy shaking the bottle to make sounds. Different dry products will make different sounds, so children will enjoy experimenting with how different sounds are made. ◆ Children will also enjoy listening to music and shaking out the rhythm.
Health and safety	◆ The adults must check that all the bottles are undamaged and that there are no sharp edges. ◆ It is very important that the adults watch children closely when they handle the dry products to make sure that they do not put any into their mouths. ◆ The adults should make sure that the lids are very tightly closed/sealed, so that they do not fly off when the bottle is shaken.

Table 10.2 Sample activity plan

Summary

In this unit you have learnt that:

◆ there are many musical activities and games that young children can learn from and enjoy
◆ there are lots of different instruments that adults can make with young children
◆ activity plans help you to think about the skills that children could learn when doing the activity, and what the adult can do to make sure that the activity is enjoyable and safe.

Chapter 11

CFC 24 Practical health and safety when with young children

What you will learn in this unit

You will gain an understanding of:

◆ the meanings of symbols and instructions on young children's equipment and toys
◆ health and safety instructions
◆ health and safety rules, guidelines and instructions when taking children out of the setting
◆ health and safety equipment and safety features
◆ potential hazards to young children in the home
◆ how to make sure that young children stay safe in the home
◆ safety equipment and controls which help to keep young children safe outside the setting
◆ possible fire hazards to young children and adults in a home.

LO1 Health and safety guidelines and instructions

1.1 Children's equipment and toys

All toys and equipment given to children should be checked to make sure that they are both safe and suitable for the age of the child. Checking toys for damage, such as cracks or loose parts will help to keep children safe when playing.

Important words

Potential hazard – a possible problem or danger.

Fire hazard – something that may cause a fire.

There are many **health and safety symbols** to look for when choosing safe and suitable toys. Look back at Table 7.2 in Chapter 7, Supporting babies to play (CFC 17), for information on the different safety symbols and logos.

Task

Make a booklet called 'Health and safety for children'. Use this booklet to complete all the assessment tasks in this unit.

Important words

Health and safety guidelines/guidance – information about how to stay healthy and safe.

Health and safety instructions – rules that are given to follow to keep people safe.

Health and safety symbols – signs or stamps used to show that something is safe to use.

Assessment task 1

Look at safety labels and instructions on toys and equipment. In your booklet, draw the symbols that you find on three items and write down what you learn from the label or the instructions.

1.2 Safe use of household cleaning products and chemicals

Household **cleaning products** and chemicals can be very dangerous. All containers have warnings if what is inside could cause harm, and instructions telling you what to do in an emergency. Some cleaning products or chemicals can be harmful when breathed in. If certain chemicals come into contact with your eyes, skin or are swallowed, they can do harm, make you very ill or may even kill you.

Figure 11.1 Cleaning products should always be kept away from children

Important words

Cleaning products – liquids or powders used to clean floors, cookers or carpets, for example.

Task

Write a list of products that you often use at home which could cause harm to children, for example, shampoo (if swallowed).

Young children may see brightly coloured washing tablets or cleaning products and think they look tasty, so put them in their mouths, but these products contain dangerous chemicals and can cause serious harm to children. All cleaning products *must* be kept away from children in a place the child cannot reach and, if possible, be kept in a locked cupboard.

Here are some very important safety points to remember:

◆ Read the labels on the products you use in your home and in the setting.
◆ Look for these words and phrases on bottles and packaging: 'Caution', 'Warning', 'Poison', 'Danger', 'Keep out of reach of children'.
◆ Keep these products in a safe place, locked away from children.
◆ Always put the lid straight back on after using the product.
◆ Do not pour cleaning products into other containers, such as an empty juice bottle, because someone else, especially a child, might think it is safe to drink.
◆ Some cleaning products can give off dangerous chemicals if they are mixed with other products, for example, if bleach and vinegar-based products are mixed together, a dangerous chlorine gas is given off.

Figure 11.2 shows some examples of symbols and instructions that can be found on the side of cleaning products.

Figure 11.2 Safety symbols and instructions which are shown on cleaning products

Assessment task 2

Look at the label on a household cleaning product. In the booklet you have made, write down the name of the product and copy the important information from the label. Figure 11.3 on the next page (page 89) gives an example.

CACHE Level 1 Caring for Children

Warnings:	Danger: Harmful if swallowed. This product contains sodium hydroxide. Wear long rubber gloves when using to avoid it touching the skin. Avoid contact with all skin, eyes, mucous membranes (mouth, lips/nose) and clothing.
Severe health effects:	From inhalation (breathing in) this product. Causes burns on contact. Eye contact: Causes burns to eyes on contact. Skin contact: causes burns to skin on contact. Ingestion: harmful if swallowed. May cause burns to mouth, throat and stomach.
First Aid:	• If this product splashes in EYES: immediately rinse eyes with water and continue rinsing eyes for 15 minutes. Call a doctor if necessary. • If this product touches the SKIN: rinse skin immediately and remove clothing that has the product on. Wash thoroughly with soap and water and continue rinsing with water for ten minutes. If the skin is damaged, see a doctor. • If you breathe in the fumes from this product, known as INHALATION: move person to fresh air. Call a doctor if the person is at all unwell. • If you swallow this product, known as INGESTION: DO NOT make the person sick. Rinse mouth thoroughly with water, drink water or milk. Call a doctor immediately.

Figure 11.3 A sample cleaning product label

1.3 Outdoor safety for children

There are many dangers in the world around us. It is very important to think about these dangers when taking children outdoors.

Water hazards
Children should always be closely watched when they are anywhere near water, so that there is no danger of children drowning.

Dogs and dog toilet areas
Adults should look out for soiled areas, and never allow children to touch dogs or other animals that do not belong to them.

Roads and traffic
Always make sure that adults help children to cross the road safely. Teaching children about road safety is important.

Litter (broken glass, needles, sharp objects)
Adults should safely remove any sharp or dangerous objects, and never allow children to pick up or touch any litter that is sharp or dangerous.

Poisonous plants
Adults should be aware of any harmful plants and remove them if possible. Children should not touch or taste any seeds, berries or leaves.

Uneven surfaces and slopes
Children should be reminded to walk carefully, looking where they are walking.

2.1, 2.2 Hazards and safety features in the home

Although we might think that our homes are safe places for children, every year many children are seriously injured or die because of accidents in the home.

> **Important words**
>
> **Safety features** – a part of an object that makes it safe to use, such as seatbelts in a car.
>
> **Safety equipment** – equipment that keeps adults and children safe, such as car seats or fire blankets.

Most of the accidents that happen to children in the home can be avoided. Adults need to take care to keep children safe in the home by supervising them carefully and never leaving them alone if there is a chance that a child could be harmed.

Being tidy and organised can help to keep children safe. Adults are more likely to spot hazards if the home is well organised. Table 11.1 includes some household hazards, the associated risk, and the **safety equipment** needed to create a safe place for children.

Hazard/task	Risk to children	Safety equipment needed and ways to reduce the chance of children being injured or becoming seriously ill
Trailing wires and cables	Tripping up or getting the cord caught round their neck and being strangled	Keep wires and cables tidy and away from children. Use a **cable tidy** (which is cheap to buy). Never have cables trailing across the floor.
Plug sockets	Poking items or fingers into the socket, receiving a serious electric shock which could cause death	When the sockets are not being used, cover them with a **socket safety cover**.
Bath time	Drowning in the water, being scalded by very hot water, serious burns could cause scarring or even death to a child	*Never* leave children alone at bath time even for a minute; they should always be supervised. Always put the cold water into the bath first so that if the child climbs in before you have checked the temperature, they are less likely to be scalded. Use a **thermometer** to check the water temperature, which should be between 37°C and 38°C.

Table 11.1 Safety equipment required to avoid hazards in the home

Hazard/task	Risk to children	Safety equipment needed and ways to reduce the chance of children being injured or becoming seriously ill
Sleep time	Suffocation or falling out of bed	Babies and young children should always sleep in a cot so that they do not roll out. Children should not have cords or ties on their clothing as these could wrap around their necks and choke them. Sheets and blankets must not cover a baby's head. Place a baby at the bottom of a cot and then tuck the blankets in, so that the baby does not slip under the covers.
Hot drinks	Children can be badly burned if they pull a hot drink onto themselves	Adults should never drink hot drinks near children. When putting drinks down, they should be placed at the back of the work surface, out of the reach of children.
Toys and equipment	Children can trip and fall over toys which are lying around on the floor Children can pull toys and equipment onto themselves if they are stacked up high	Tidy away toys and equipment that are not being used. Place toys and equipment tidily in cupboards or in **storage boxes**. Make a space for children to play safely.
Stairs	Children can fall downstairs or trip over toys left lying on the stairs	Never leave anything on stairs. If children are young, fit **safety gates** to the top and bottom of the stairs, to stop children climbing up and down the stairs without an adult.
High chairs	Children can fall from high chairs and be injured	Always use a **safety harness** and supervise children.
Pans on cookers	Children can pull the pans onto themselves or touch the heat and be burned	Use a **cooker guard**, which will stop children from touching the heat or the pans.

Table 11.1 Safety equipment required to avoid hazards in the home *(Continued)*

In the booklet you made, write a list of five hazards in the home. For each one, say what you will need to do to keep the child safe.

Illness or death can be caused by children touching or playing with dangerous products, or by swallowing harmful chemicals, such as medicines or cleaning products.

Medicine and tablet safety

Medicines are often brightly coloured and children may think that they are sweets, but they can be very dangerous if eaten. It is *very* important to keep all medicines and tablets out of the reach of children.

Too much medicine or the wrong medicine can harm or even kill. Medicines that are meant for adults can make children very ill.

Here are some very important safety points to remember:

◆ Medicines should be stored in a locked cupboard or box and kept out of the reach of children.
◆ Medicine bottles should have child-safety screw tops.
◆ The correct amount of medicine should be given at the right times.

Figure 11.4 Medicines must be kept away from children

◆ Always keep medicines in the packet or container that they came in.
◆ Read and keep any labels or instruction leaflets that come with the medicine – this will give you information about what to do if there is a problem.
◆ Never give prescribed medicines to other people, even if they seem to have a similar illness.
◆ Old or out of date/expired medicines and tablets should be taken back to the chemist, so that they can be destroyed.
◆ Do not put medicines down the sink or toilet. They can poison the water and make people and animals sick.

2.3 Safety equipment outside the setting

Children can be badly injured if they are not looked after properly when taken outdoors. Figure 11.5 shows some ways to keep children safe when outdoors.

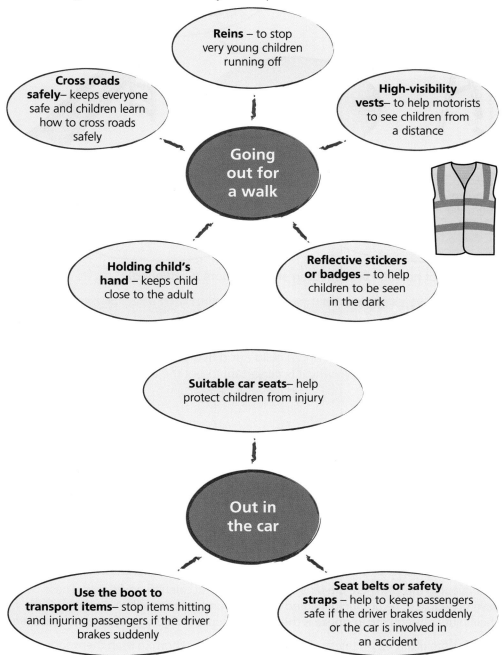

Figure 11.5 Examples of how to keep children safe outdoors

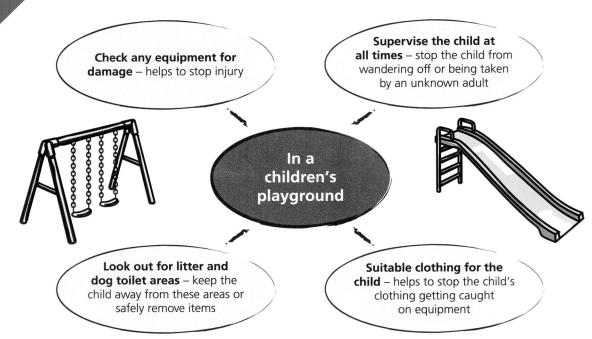

Check any equipment for damage – helps to stop injury

Supervise the child at all times – stop the child from wandering off or being taken by an unknown adult

In a children's playground

Look out for litter and dog toilet areas – keep the child away from these areas or safely remove items

Suitable clothing for the child – helps to stop the child's clothing getting caught on equipment

Figure 11.5 Examples of how to keep children safe outdoors *(Continued)*

Assessment task 4

Find out about car safety for children. Cut out pictures of car seats suitable for a baby aged one month and a child aged five years, and stick them into your booklet. Write down why it is important to get the right type of car seat for a child.

Assessment task 5

In your booklet, write about how you can keep a child safe on a walk to the local shop. Include some of the potential hazards and the ways to keep children safe.

LO3 Fire safety in the home

Every year in the UK, there are tens of thousands of accidental house fires. These cause several people to be burned or injured every day and some people die as a result of their injuries. Breathing in smoke is the greatest cause of injury or death in a house fire.

Children are often very interested in fire, so it is essential both to keep them safe and to try to teach them about the dangers of fire.

It is very important to think about fire safety and, whenever possible, to remove the risk of children and adults being injured by fire.

3.1 Recommended fire safety equipment

There are a few pieces of **recommended** equipment that can help to keep children and adults safe if a fire breaks out in the home:

> **Important words**
>
> **Recommended** – suggested because it is important.

- A **working smoke alarm** that is tested weekly. This will sound loudly if smoke is in the air and allows people in the house to get out quickly and safely.
- A **fire blanket** kept in the kitchen can be used to put over the top of burning pans to put out the flames.
- **Fire extinguishers**: there are three main types of fire extinguishers: powder, water and foam (depending on the type of fire). Fire extinguishers are only recommended to be used by people who have been trained to use them safely.
- A **working telephone** should be available to call 999 to contact the emergency services in the event of a fire.
- A **well-fitted fireguard** around a fireplace will stop children and adults getting too close to the fire, so that they do not get burnt and their clothes do not catch fire.

Assessment task 6

In your booklet, list the fire safety equipment that is recommended for use in the home.

3.2 Fire hazards in the home

There are many ways that fires can be started accidentally within the home:

- **Cigarettes**: more people die in fires caused by lit cigarettes, matches and lighters than in fires caused by anything else. Children should be kept away from cigarettes and matches.
- **Candles** and lit decorations cause a growing number of house fires and should not be used around children.
- **Overloaded sockets**: too many electrical appliances plugged into one socket can overload it, which can lead to electrical equipment catching fire. Children should never touch an electric socket or cable.

- **Cooking**: more than half of fires in the home start because of something to do with cooking. Children should *never* be left alone in a kitchen when cooking is taking place.
- **Gas and coal fires**: although it is unusual for these heating appliances to cause house fires, children are at a high risk of being burned if they get too close to them. A fireguard should always be used when a fire of any type is lit.

Assessment task 7

In your booklet, write down three fire hazards in the home.

Figure 11.6 Fire safety equipment for the home

3.3 What to do in the event of a fire

It is important that adults think about what to do if a fire breaks out in the home, especially if it is during the night.

Make your home safe for children

The Government has given specific advice about keeping children safe from fire:

◆ Do not leave children on their own in a room where there is a fire risk.
◆ Keep matches, lighters and candles in a place where children cannot see or reach them. Put child locks on cupboards that contain these items.
◆ Put a child-proof fireguard in front of an open fire or heater.
◆ Do not let children play or leave toys near a fire or heater.
◆ Keep portable heaters in a safe place where they cannot be knocked over.
◆ Never leave children alone in the kitchen when you are cooking, and never let them play near the cooker.
◆ Make sure electrical appliances are switched off when they are not being used.

A plan

It is important to have a plan so that if a fire breaks out, you do not panic. The plan should include:

◆ working out how you would safely get everyone out of your home if there was a fire, and making sure everyone in the building knows the plan (including visitors and babysitters)
◆ letting children hear the smoke/fire alarm so that they know what it sounds like and what they should do if they hear the alarm
◆ practising getting out of the building quickly with any children
◆ keeping all doors and passages clear at all times of the day and night
◆ checking for fire hazards in your home before you go to bed; it takes longer to become aware of a fire when you are asleep.

Action

If a fire breaks out, follow these guidelines:

- If the smoke or fire alarm sounds, you should quickly and safely get everyone out of the building.
- If anyone is trapped upstairs, they should close the door and put clothes or blankets under the door so that dangerous smoke stays out of the room. They should move close to the window so that they can be seen by the emergency services.
- Call the emergency services by dialling 999 immediately. Try to stay calm and give your address and details of what is happening.
- Do not go back into the building until you are told it is safe to do so.

Assessment task 8

In your booklet, write a plan for how to get children out of the building safely if there is a fire.

Summary

In this unit you have learnt that:

- safety symbols help us to choose safe and suitable toys and equipment for children
- cleaning product labels show important information about their safe use
- adults have a big role in keeping children safe, both indoors and outdoors
- there is a range of equipment to help keep children safe, both indoors and outdoors
- fires in the home cause injury and death to many children and adults every year
- adults should plan and practise how to get children and adults out of the building safely if there was a fire.

What you will learn in this unit

You will gain an understanding of:

◆ what a Forest School is
◆ how being outdoors helps children to be healthy
◆ the places that children can safely learn outdoors
◆ ways in which children can learn in the outdoor environment
◆ what kinds of skills children can develop when they are learning outside.

LO1 Forest Schools

1.1 What is a Forest School?

A Forest School is a school where children spend most of the day outside, whatever the weather. All the learning that would usually take place inside a school, such as counting, matching and sorting, role play and creative activities, takes places outdoors. Children play and learn by using their senses to explore the outdoors. Most Forest Schools are in areas where there are lots of trees, bushes and wooded areas.

Task

Thinking about your school or college environment, make a list of the things around you that help you to feel comfortable and able to learn, for example, lights, desks and tables.

The main features of a Forest School are as follows:

◆ The children spend most of the day learning in a woodland or forest outdoors, instead of inside in a classroom.
◆ Children spend time exploring and looking at nature while they are outside. They can touch the leaves and trees instead of just looking at them in pictures.

- Children also have the opportunity to climb trees, and to make dens to play in and keep dry in the rain.
- Children are outdoors even in the rain and snow; they just have to wear the right clothes to keep themselves warm and dry.
- Children can see the changes through the seasons, for example, in springtime most trees begin to blossom and the forest becomes green.
- Children learn lots of new social skills. This includes learning to communicate with other children when they are doing an activity together, for example, deciding what materials to use when they are building a den.
- Children learn teamwork skills, for example, deciding which route to take when they are walking through the forest. The children will all have to agree to go the same way so that everyone stays together and no child is left to wander off alone.
- Children have the chance to explore outdoors in the fresh air. They will be able to experience the weather, for example, feeling the rain bouncing on their waterproof jackets or seeing the wind blowing the leaves around.
- There is usually some sort of shelter where children can relax.
- Children are able to use a range of tools, such as spades, saws and ropes.

Assessment task 1

Design a poster to show the main features that can be found in a Forest School.

Figure 12.1 The natural world is a rich environment for children's learning

LO2 Choosing an outdoor learning environment

2.1, 2.2 Different types of outdoor learning environments

There are many outdoor areas that children will enjoy exploring and where they can learn about the environment. Children can learn lots of different skills and gain knowledge about the world they live in from being in different types of outdoor areas. Figure 12.2 shows examples of different outdoor areas, and Table 12.1 explores how the outdoor environment can boost children's learning.

Figure 12.2 Different types of outdoor areas

Outdoor area where learning takes place	What does this area look like?	What can children learn in the area?	What new skills can children develop in the area?
Woodland areas	These are areas mostly covered with trees, shrubs and flowers.	Children can learn about the seasons and how the woodland changes. They can learn about insects, birds and woodland animals, such as woodlice, beetles, badgers, foxes and owls.	Children can learn how to walk carefully without damaging the woodland. They can learn to safely climb and move through the wooded area. They can learn how to make dens, build shelters and use tools safely.

Table 12.1 How the outdoor environment can boost children's learning

Outdoor area where learning takes place	What does this area look like?	What can children learn in the area?	What new skills can children develop in the area?
Fields and meadows	Fields are large areas of grassland and can sometimes be used to grow crops. Meadows are usually left to grow naturally and can be full of wild flowers. 	Children can learn by looking at the crops and flowers, and observing how they grow and change. They can use their senses by gently touching and smelling the wild flowers. They can learn about the seasons and how the fields and meadows change. They can learn about how things grow, and about insects, birds and animals, such as field mice, swallows and hedgehogs.	Children can learn how to walk carefully without damaging the fields and meadows. They can learn to watch bugs and insects without damaging the area in which they live.
Ponds and streams	Ponds are small areas of water which can be created naturally or be man-made. Streams are small, narrow rivers.	Ponds and streams are good places to find many living animals. Children can find insects or plants in or around the pond or stream. They can observe the birds and other animals that visit the water for rest and food. They can look for fish if the pond or stream is large enough. They can learn the life cycle of butterflies and frogs.	Children can learn to use fishing nets to look at pond life. They can balance on rocks if it is safe to do so. They can use magnifying glasses to look at tiny pond life. They can learn how to be responsible for their own safety by following rules about safe play. An example of this is when children are free to play by the water edge as long as they are wearing a float jacket. They can learn how to use tools safely.

Table 12.1 How the outdoor environment can boost children's learning *(Continued)*

Outdoor area where learning takes place	What does this area look like?	What can children learn in the area?	What new skills can children develop in the area?
Forests	These are large areas covered with trees. Some forests have trees that are very tall, which means that they block out the sun and very little sunlight gets to the ground.	Children can learn about how trees change through the seasons, and which leaves and fruits belong to different trees. They can learn by walking through the forest, watching what is happening around them. They can use all of their senses to learn about the forest area. They can smell the woodland, listen to the animals and birds and feel the textures of the forest.	Children can learn how to use magnifying glasses to closely watch how bugs and insects move. They can learn how to make shelters and dens. They can practise tree climbing and log balancing. Learning how to navigate through a thick forest without getting lost is a good skill to learn. They can track signs of forest animals, such as foxes or badgers, and use tools safely.

Table 12.1 How the outdoor environment can boost children's learning *(Continued)*

2.3 Safety issues in an outdoor environment

Safety is very important and must be thought about at all times. All activities and forest areas are checked for dangers by staff: this is called **risk assessing**.

◆ Children must never be left alone and should always be supervised closely by adults.
◆ When using tools, such as spades and saws, children are shown how to use them carefully and safely.
◆ When safely making fires, children are watched closely by the adults.
◆ At all times children are encouraged to think about what they are doing and how to do it safely to ensure that they do not get hurt.

Figure 12.3 on the next page (page 104) explores safety issues and things that adults need to remember.

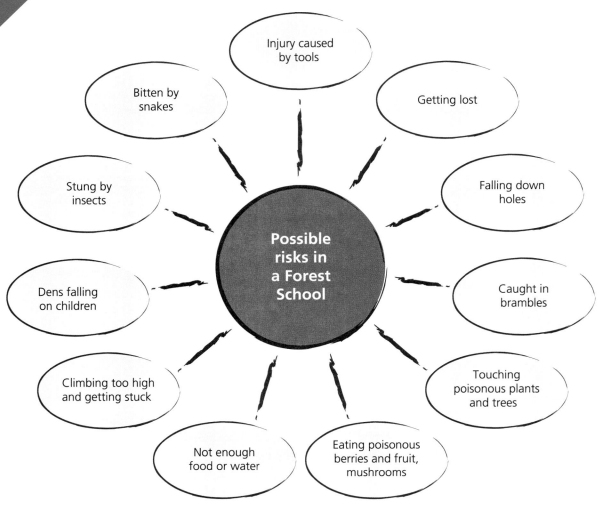

Figure 12.3 Possible risks in a Forest School

3.1, 3.2 Outdoor projects

There are many projects that can be enjoyed by children in outdoor areas. These could include the following:

◆ learning the life cycles of butterflies or frogs
◆ observing the woodland through the seasons
◆ building a den
◆ building a dam in a stream
◆ planting and growing
◆ weather watching.

Task

In small groups, write down other projects that would be suitable to do outdoors with young children.

Projects can be both enjoyable and full of new learning experiences for children. Projects can last for just a few hours or up to a few months. For example, a short project could be building a den, but a much longer project could be recording weather patterns over a few months.

Figure 12.4 Building a den provides many opportunities for learning

Assessment task 3

Using one of the projects you have written down or one taken from the list above:

1 Write a description of the project, saying what the children will do.
2 Write a list of what children might learn during this project.
3 Write down two skills which children might learn during the project.

3.3, 4.1 Benefits to children of learning outdoors

From completing this unit, you will have learnt that there are many benefits to children of learning in different outdoor areas. Children are learning by using all of their senses and are developing new skills. These could be physical skills, such as tree climbing, social skills such as teamwork to build a den, learning new words to develop their language skills, or learning about the world around them to support their intellectual development.

In the outdoor areas, children usually feel they have more freedom and space to run around and explore. This can give children a sense of positive **emotional wellbeing**.

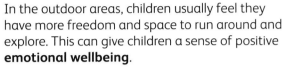

Important words

Emotional wellbeing – feeling happy in yourself and feeling positive.

Assessment task 4

Design a poster using pictures or drawings to show all the benefits to children from learning outdoors. (You could use the table and project you have just done to get your information, as well as looking on the internet or in magazines.)

Summary

In this unit you have learnt that:

◆ there are many different types of outdoor areas where children can explore and learn

◆ Forest Schools can be very interesting places for children to learn new skills

◆ adults should think carefully about children's safety when they are in outdoor areas

◆ the outdoor area is a good place for adults to support children's learning

◆ there are many benefits to children of learning in outdoor areas

◆ young children can learn lots of new things from outdoor activities when adults support their learning.

Chapter 13

CFC 26 Craft activities for young children

What you will learn in this unit

You will gain an understanding of:

◆ craft activities which can be suitable for children (aged six months to five years)
◆ the benefits of craft activities for young children
◆ the health and safety risks that must be considered when providing craft activities for young children
◆ the adult's role in keeping children safe during craft activities.

LO1 Benefits of craft activities

1.1, 1.2 Craft activities for young children

Craft activities are enjoyed by most young children. They can be an interesting and fun way to spend time with other children and adults. Very young children often like to use paints and crayons at home and use glue and paper to make pictures at playgroups. In the early years setting, children might be given different-sized boxes, paints and shiny materials so that they can make a model of a robot or car, for example.

When choosing a craft activity to do with a young child, it is very important to make sure that it is suitable for the child's age and ability; you have to consider what they can manage to do. For example, a baby of eight months cannot yet use a pair of scissors, so should be given another type of craft activity to do.

Important words

Craft activity – making something with your hands.

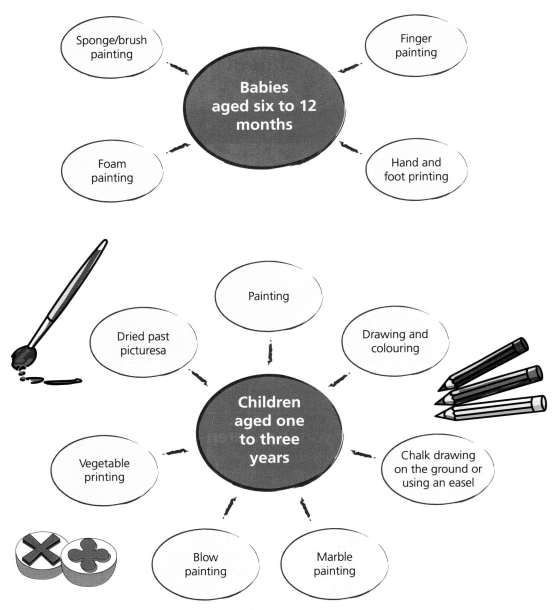

Figure 13.1 Suitable craft activities for different ages

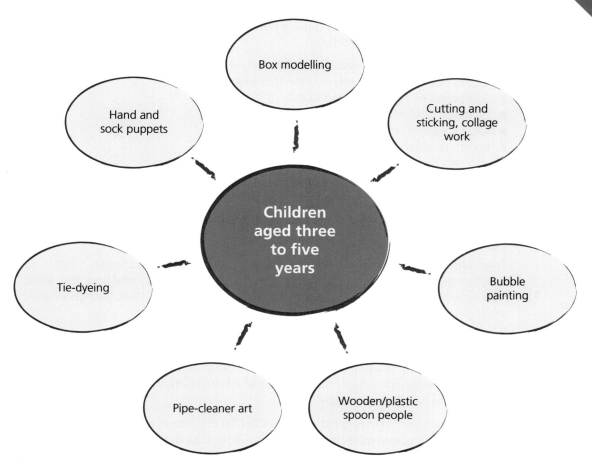

Figure 13.1 Suitable craft activities for different ages *(Continued)*

Assessment task 1a

1 In pairs, think of some more craft activities suitable for:
   ◆ a baby aged between six and 12 months
   ◆ a young child aged between one and two years
   ◆ a child aged between three and five years.
2 Write a short description of one craft activity for each age group.
3 Think about what the children would need to do the activity and the steps they would take to complete it.

Adults must make sure that they provide babies and young children with the correct equipment to complete the activity.

The equipment will depend on the craft activity that has been chosen. For example, a vegetable printing activity will need the following:
◆ a selection of vegetables and fruit
◆ paints of different colours in wide bowls or on plates
◆ large sheets of white or colour paper
◆ aprons or old shirts.

LO3 What young children can learn from craft activities

1.3, 3.1 The benefits of craft activities and what children can learn

There are many benefits for children when they take part in craft activities. Craft activities give babies and young children the chance to get messy and have fun. Most craft activities help children to develop good hand—eye co-ordination, such as when they hold a crayon and move it carefully around the page.

Craft activities can help to build children's confidence and self-esteem (see page 164 for definition/meaning), as they can feel proud of the pictures they make. This can be a good time to talk to children and develop their social skills. The activities can also help to support their language development, finding words to describe what they are doing, for example, 'the dough feels squishy'.

Craft activities also provide great opportunities for children to learn new things, such as how long paint takes to dry on the paper, or how much glue you need to use. Children may use different-coloured crayons or different-shaped paper; the adult can use this as an opportunity to support the learning of colours, shapes and even counting.

When planning craft activities, it is important that adults think about the children in the group and ensure that everyone is included. For example, if you are asking children to draw or paint a picture of themselves, it is important to give the children colours that match all hair, eye and skin colours.

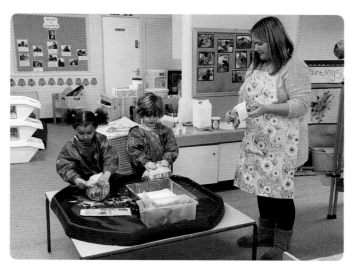

Figure 13.2 Craft activities can boost children's confidence

Some children may need extra support to take part in certain activities, for example, a child who uses a wheelchair may need more space to get to the table where the activity is set out.

Assessment task 1b

In pairs, make a list of all the new things that could be learned through doing the craft activities chosen in the last task. Copy and complete Table 13.1.

Age of child	Craft activity	Learning opportunities

Table 13.1 Learning opportunities provided by craft activities

LO2 Health and safety during craft activities

2.1, 2.2 Health and safety risks during craft activities and how to deal with them

There are some health and safety risks with craft activities for young children, which need to be thought about by adults before doing the activity. These could be things that could cause an accident or injure a child.

Task

In pairs, write a list of equipment that children might use during a craft activity and then think about some of the dangers of this equipment when used by children. For example, a pair of scissors can be used safely with no injury, however:

◆ scissors can be dangerous, even ones especially made for young children
◆ scissors are often made from a hard material and are long, thin and slightly pointed
◆ scissors may cause an injury if a young child puts them inside their own mouth, or if one child uses the scissors to poke another child.

!

Important words

Health and safety risks – any harm or injury that may take place.

A risk is not something that would definitely cause injury or harm during an activity, but it is something that should be thought about and considered by the adult.

Health and safety risks during craft activities

- Glue on skin, sticking fingers together
- Paint going in a child's eye
- Spilled water on the floor, making it slippery
- A child putting foam into their mouth
- A child putting a marble in their mouth, or choking on a small piece of dried pasta
- Putting pipe-cleaners up noses or in ears
- A child eating fruit or vegetables that had been used for painting

Figure 13.3 Possible **health and safety risks** during craft activities

2.3 Supporting a child to carry out craft activities safely

During any activity with young children, the adult should be aware of accidents that may happen. Even with careful planning and thought, certain things can go wrong. Children often put things in their mouths or use equipment in the wrong way, such as waving a paintbrush like a toy sword. It is important that children are watched carefully when they are doing any sort of craft activity, so that if the child begins to use equipment in the wrong way or spills something, you can safely deal with the situation.

Always make sure that the tools and equipment are in good condition and suitable for the craft activity.

Adults working with babies and young children need to think about health and safety risks before doing an activity with them. When a risk has been identified by the adult, they can then think of ways to deal with the risk and stop an accident from happening.

Assessment task 2

Copy and complete Table 13.2, which lists health and safety risks when providing craft activities, how to deal with these risks and ways in which the adult can support young children.

Health and safety risks when providing craft activities for young children	How to deal with the health and safety risks	The support which children might need when doing the craft activity
Using sharp scissors	Make sure that safety scissors are being used. Make sure that left-handed children have the appropriate scissors.	Discuss safe ways of using scissors with the children. Observe the activity to make sure that the scissors are being used correctly.

Table 13.2 Health and safety risks during craft activities

Summary

In this unit you have learnt that:

- craft activities are enjoyed by most young children
- there are many different types of craft activities that are suitable for young children, and adults need to make sure that the activity is right for the age of the child
- children can learn lots of things when enjoying craft activities, including counting, colours and shapes
- adults should always watch children carefully to keep them safe during craft activities
- it is important to think about any possible risk of children being harmed during the activity and, if necessary, change the activity so that it is safe
- some children may need extra support to be able to join in the activity.

What you will learn in this unit

You will gain an understanding of:

◆ the features of a positive learning environment

◆ how play can help children's learning and development

◆ the ways in which play activities should meetchildren's individual needs and avoid stereotyping and discrimination.

LO1 Features of a positive learning environment

1.1 How settings can be positive learning environments

A **positive learning environment** can be created both indoors (for example, a playroom at a toddler group or a day nursery) and outdoors (for example, outside in a woodland or garden area).

Features of a positive learning environment

The **features** that make a positive learning environment are very different for indoor and outdoor settings. Figure 14.1 (a and b) highlights some of the features of indoor and outdoor environments.

Important words

Positive learning environment – a room or place that supports children's learning.

Features of a setting – the appearance and description of a room or place.

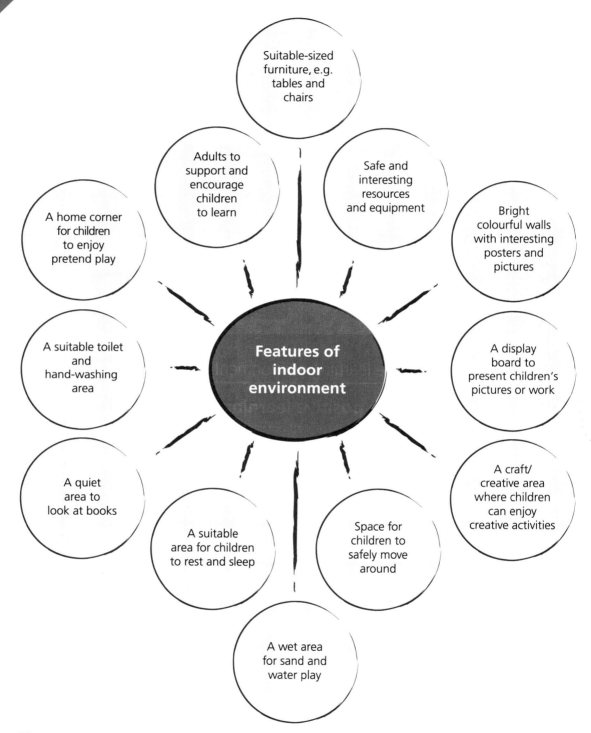

Figure 14.1a Features of indoor environments

CACHE Level 1 Caring for Children

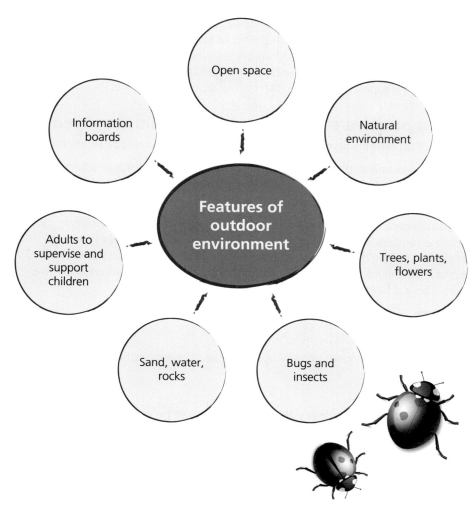

Figure 14.1b Features of outdoor environments

Adult support

It is very important that adults are interested in what the children are doing, and support children to have fun, enjoy the activities and stay safe. Adults can talk to children and ask lots of questions to get them to think about what they already know. It is important that adults show interest in what the children are doing and try to make it fun because this will encourage the children to play for longer and provide more opportunity for them to learn new things. Adults should not take over the child's play; if the child asks for help or is struggling to do an activity, the adult can help or show them how to do it without completing the activity for them.

Adults should support children to stay safe. However, all children need to take some risks, so the adult needs to make sure the child is as safe as possible while enabling them to do this. For example, when children are learning to climb up a rope during PE lessons, there is the risk of falling so the adult *must* ensure there are no sharp objects to fall onto around the rope and place a crash mat underneath the rope.

1.2 How a positive environment helps children to learn

The features of an environment are important for children for many different reasons.

In a positive environment, there should be plenty of opportunities for children to play and learn and to feel safe and well cared for. The environment should enable *all* children to feel included and to develop and learn.

Positive environments help children to understand that all children are different, but that everyone matters. For example, a 'Welcome to our nursery' poster showing children playing can be displayed on a nursery wall. The poster should show a mix of boys and girls, children from different ethnic backgrounds and children who have disabilities. This will help all children to feel they are welcome.

Task

In small groups, write down other ways to make all children feel welcome in the nursery.

If children feel welcome in a nursery, they will feel happy. Children who feel happy will be more likely to enjoy trying new activities, so they will learn more from taking part. Children who feel uncomfortable and unhappy will not want to take part in activities, so they will miss out on learning new things. It is the responsibility of the adult to make all children feel welcome. It is also their job to make sure the environment is a fun place to be. They can help to achieve this by providing a wide range of interesting toys and activities and by putting up colourful and interesting displays.

Task

In small groups, look at Tables 14.1 and 14.2, showing the features of indoor and outdoor settings. Copy the tables and fill in the blank cells.

Features of indoor settings	How the features can help children's learning
Suitable-sized furniture	Children are comfortable, so they will be able to concentrate on their activities. Children can safely get on and off the chairs, so they can learn to be independent.
Interesting posters and pictures on the wall	Children will enjoy looking at the posters and pictures and learn new things. The pictures might be a way of introducing children to new words or starting discussions with the children.
A display board	
A craft/creative area	
A suitable area for children to rest and sleep	
A wet area for sand and water play	This area will enable children to play with sand and water safely, so that if any goes on the floor children will not slip and fall. They can learn about how the texture of sand changes as the water is added to it.
A suitable toilet and handwashing area	This will enable children to wash hands after messy play and be able to use the toilet so that they can become independent.

Table 14.1 Features of indoor settings

Features of outdoor settings	How the features can help children's learning
Different types of weather and changes in temperature	Children learn about what the weather feels like, such as wind and rain. Children understand about wearing suitable clothes to keep warm, cool or dry.
Trees to climb, logs to balance on	This provides risk and challenge. Children learn about keeping themselves safe.
Dens to build and use	Children learn about construction through play. They learn how to use tools safely.
Sand, water and rocks	
Information boards	These show pictures and give information about the environment and wildlife.
Bugs and insects to discover	

Table 14.2 Features of outdoor settings

Assessment task 1

In pairs, design a room or outside play area which children aged between three and four years may enjoy using. Draw and label all the features that **contribute** to your positive learning environment. When deciding on the important features, think about how each of the features might help and encourage children to learn.

Important words

Contribute – add to.

LO2 How play can help children's learning

2.1 How play supports early learning

Play is a very important part of children's learning and development. It is through play that children use their senses to develop new skills and learn about the world around them.

When children play, they are practising skills they have already learnt and developing new ones. When children play together, they are learning how to share as well as having fun, being occupied by what they are doing and burning energy while running and playing sports. A great deal of learning takes place that perhaps is not so obvious at first.

Play can support children's development in the following areas:

◆ **physical** – many play activities help children to learn to do things with their body
◆ **social** – many play activities can help children to relate to others
◆ **emotional** – many play activities can help children to understand how they feel
◆ **intellectual** – many play activities can help children to develop their thinking
◆ **language** – many play activities help children to learn new words.

Figure 14.3 on the next page (page 122) shows examples of play activities that support different areas of development.

Figure 14.2 Playing together supports learning

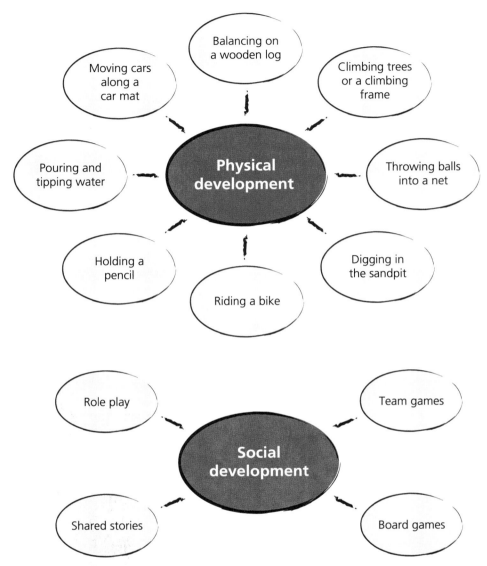

Figure 14.3 Examples of how learning and development can be supported by play activities

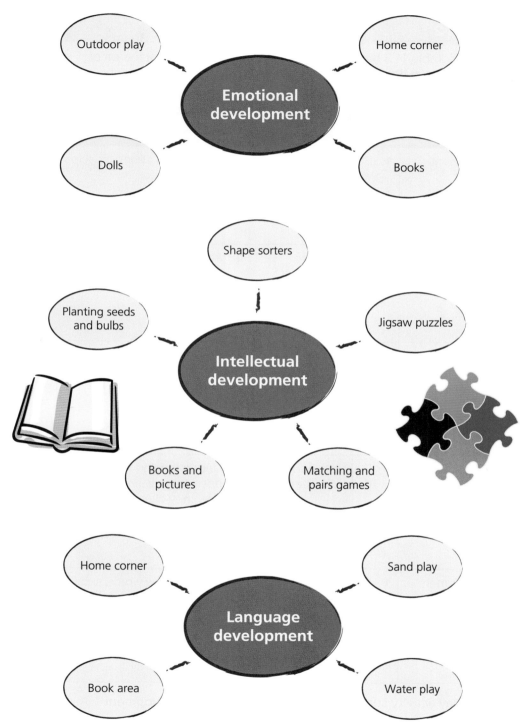

Figure 14.3 How play supports different areas of development *(Continued)*

Assessment task 2

Copy and complete Table 14.3 by suggesting a second activity for each area of development. Write down how it helps children's learning and development.

Area of development	Play activity	How the play activity helps children's learning and development
Physical development	**1** Balancing on a wooden log **2**	**1** Developing strong muscles and good balance. **2**
Social development	**1** Board games **2**	**1** Agreeing the rules, turn taking and sharing the dice. **2**
Emotional development	**1** Outdoor play **2**	**1** Feeling proud when they have climbed higher in the tree, running around and feeling free. **2**
Intellectual development	**1** Planting seeds and caring for them **2**	**1** Understanding what seeds need to grow and observing how they change as they grow. **2**
Language development	**1** Sand play **2**	**1** Learning new words, such as 'sprinkle', 'pat', 'scoop', 'tip', 'rake', talking to each other as they play. **2**

Table 14.3 How play activity supports children's learning and development

CACHE Level 1 Caring for Children

LO3 How play activities can avoid stereotyping and discrimination

3.1 Examples of stereotyping

Discrimination occurs when the environment, materials or activities are not suitable for all children. This may make some children feel left out and excluded. It is therefore essential that adults **challenge discrimination** and make sure that all children feel included. For example, if a child attends the nursery and sees pictures of families from their own cultural background in books and on posters, they will feel included and understand that their culture is valued.

Stereotyping happens when we label people or make judgements about them because of what we see or think. To help children learn not to stereotype roles in the home and wider world, they should see pictures of men and women in a variety of roles, for example men and women in a variety of roles, for example men ironing clothes or in nursing roles, or women mending cars and in engineering roles.

Figure 14.4 Girls and boys should be encouraged to play with all toys

Important words

Discrimination – an instance where an individual is disadvantaged because of a **protected characteristic**, such as disability or religion.

Protected characteristic – a specific aspect of a person's identity defined by the Equality Act and protected by law from discrimination.

Challenge discrimination – when we take action to make sure that no child feels left out or bullied because of what they can do or how they look.

Stereotyping – believing that a group of people, or a person, have a certain characteristic, which might not be accurate.

Protected characteristic – a specific aspect of a person's identity defined by the Equality Act and protected by law from discrimination

Task

Copy Table 14.4 on the next page (page 126), about challenging discrimination and stereotyping in play, and fill in the blank cells.

Activity or resource	How we can make sure that this activity or resource challenges stereotyping	How we can make sure that this activity or resource challenges discrimination
Small world play	The plastic people/figures can be given different, varied and non-stereotypical roles, e.g. a girl can be driving a lorry and a boy can be shopping.	The plastic people/figures could be of different races/have different colour skin and be dressed in clothes from different cultures.
Jigsaw puzzles		
Posters		
Home corner		Have a variety of different types of cooking pots and foods, e.g. woks to cook in and plastic foods from different countries.
Dolls		
Books	Having stories and pictures of people with disabilities doing everyday activities, such as taking the bus, going to work or joining in with sports.	

Table 14.4 Ways in which to combat discrimination and stereotyping in children's play

Summary

In this unit you have learnt that:

◆ many different features of indoor and outdoor environments can support children's learning

◆ play activities can help children's physical, social, emotional, intellectual and language development

◆ having a good variety of resources and carefully planned activities will help to challenge stereotyping and discrimination.

What you will learn in this unit

You will gain an understanding of:

◆ the significance of your achievements and interests to your development

◆ your personal strengths and areas for further development

◆ your learning styles, skills, qualities and abilities

◆ how to produce an action plan to your identify personal goals

◆ using this information to make career and education choices.

LO1 What your achievements and interests mean for your development

This means thinking about how your own **achievements** and interests have helped you to develop up to now.

1.1 Describe at least two achievements and interests

Achievements

Our achievements are the things that we have successfully managed to do. For example, you may learn to swim or become good at gymnastics. Sometimes learning a new skill or understanding more about something may result in you achieving an award or getting a certificate.

Other achievements may be as simple as becoming more confident in different situations. For example, deciding to start a new college course or becoming more organised when preparing for an exam.

Task

In pairs, make a list of all your achievements in your life so far. Think about when you may have been afraid or anxious about trying something that you then successfully managed to do. Do not forget to include any qualifications, certificates or awards you have achieved.

Important words

Achievement – this is something that you successfully managed to do.

Interests

Our interests help us to make choices about college courses or future work goals. You may enjoy spending time with older adults, and this could make you think that a job working in care of older adults would suit you.

> ## Important words
>
> **Research** – finding information, for example from the internet, books or by speaking to others.

When someone has an interest, they might do some **research** to find out more about it. For example, if you enjoy keeping fit, you might contact the local sports centre to find out about fitness classes or gym membership.

1.2 How your achievements and interests have supported your development

Case study

Salina is 15 years old and lives with her dad, her three sisters and her grandmother. Ever since she was very young, Salina has enjoyed helping her grandmother in the kitchen at home. Salina feels confident in helping to cook the family meals. This interest in cooking made Salina research cookery and catering courses that were available at her local college. Salina applied for a place on a cookery course, had a successful interview with the tutor and was offered a place on the course. Salina is looking forward to starting college in September.

Assessment task 1

Copy and complete Table 15.1 to show your achievements and interests and to describe how these have supported your own development.

Achievement/Interest	Ways that this has supported my development
Example: *Learning to touch type on a computer*	*This has helped me to be able to confidently use a computer to complete school and college coursework. I can present my work in a professional way and easily make any changes.*

Table 15.1 How my achievements and interests have supported my development

Figure 15.1 Amelia used a laptop to find out about the courses at her local college

LO2 Strengths and areas for development

As well as our achievements, such as successfully completing a course, we also have things in our lives that we find difficult or need to improve.

2.1 Your strengths in skills, qualities and abilities and their importance for the future

Skills

When caring for babies and children, it is important to work professionally. This means having a wide range of **skills**, such as good communication, arriving at work on time, being clean and well-presented and following **policies and procedures** correctly.

Qualities

It is also very important to have the right **qualities** for your chosen job role. For example, when working with babies and children, it is important to be a good role model because young children will often copy the people around them. Other key qualities are being patient and caring towards others around you.

> **Important words**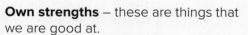
>
> **Own strengths** – these are things that we are good at.
>
> **Areas for further development** – these are things that we need to improve or get better at.
>
> **Skills** – something we are able to do well.
>
> **Policies and procedures** – these are the rules of the setting, which need to be followed at all times when working with babies and children.
>
> **Qualities** – these are good parts of our personality.

Abilities

When working with babies and children, it is essential that you are able to work well as part of a team. This means sharing ideas, supporting others in the team and making sure that all your work is done well.

> **Important words**
>
> **Abilities** – these are things we are able to do.
>
> **Make improvements** – to get better at something.

2.2 Areas for development and why and how they need to be improved

Sometimes you know that you do not have all the skills and knowledge that you need to be able to work in your chosen job role. When you are aware of the improvements that you need to make, you can decide on the best way to make these **improvements**. For example, you should ask your teacher if you do not understand something you are learning about, or if you need to improve a skill, you should make time to practise this skill. If you know that your timekeeping or communication skills are not always good, you should think about what you can do to become better at them.

> **Case study**
>
> Jenna's personal goal is to work as a football coach for young children. Jenna is occasionally late for college or forgets her ID badge, which must be worn. Jenna understands that arriving on time and being organised are skills that she must have if she wants to become a football coach. Jenna thinks about how to improve on these areas of her development; she decides she must pack her college bag the night before to make sure she has everything she needs, including her badge, and she must set her alarm an hour before she needs to leave the house.
>
> | Jenna's areas for improvement | Why they are important as a football coach | How improvements can be made by Jenna |
> |---|---|---|
> | Timekeeping | Football matches always have a certain start time. | Setting the alarm on her phone as a reminder. |
> | Forgetting her ID badge, and remembering to take this | It is important to have all the correct kit when playing sports. | Packing her bag and organising her college things the night before. |
>
> **Table 15.2** Jenna's personal development plan

2.3 Match your skills, qualities and abilities to your chosen role

When thinking about a career in childcare it is important to think about your skills, qualities and abilities. Everyone working with children should be a good role model. Children copy the behaviours of others around them, so you must always follow the rules and be respectful to others. You must show children how to be kind and caring, by being kind and caring towards them. It is important to be patient and calm around children. You must support children to manage their own behaviour by staying calm yourself when children get angry or upset.

Sometimes when deciding to work with children, we need to understand what we may need to change about ourselves. For example, if you sometimes use bad language or react to others in an aggressive way, you will need to work on changing these behaviours if you want a career with children, as these behaviours are not acceptable. If you have difficulty following rules, for example following college rules, such as arriving on time and working well in lessons, you will need to change these behaviours before you are suitable to work with children.

Task

In small groups, talk about and write down other skills, qualities and abilities you think you may need when choosing to work with babies and children.

Explain why each of these are important for:
◆ successfully completing a childcare course
◆ working well with babies and children.

Assessment task 2

1 List your own skills, qualities and abilities and describe how they will help you to successfully complete courses and be good in your chosen job role.
2 List your own areas for development (things you feel you are not doing well enough yet for the job role you chose) and describe ways to improve on these areas.

LO3 How learning style influences career and education choices

3.1 Own learning style and how it influences your choices

Your own **learning style** is how you best learn something new; you may have more than one learning style that you use.

Case study

Courtney works with young children in a nursery and her supervisor has asked her to make some playdough with the children. This is something that Courtney has not done before. If Courtney is a **visual learner**, she may go online to see how dough is made and copy this. If she is an **auditory learner**, Courtney may ask her supervisor how to make it and listen to what she tells her. If Courtney learns best by **reading and writing**, she may look in a book for instructions and then write a plan. If Courtney is a **kinaesthetic learner**, she may use the ingredients to have a go herself before doing the activity with the children.

Task

Think about how *you* would best learn how to make playdough for the first time. This may help you to understand what your learning style(s) may be.

Important words

Learning style – this is the way we learn best; we may have more than one learning style.

Visual learner – you learn best by looking at diagrams and symbols.

Auditory learner – you learn best by listening to information or taking part in group discussions, for example.

Read and write – you learn best by reading information and taking notes.

Kinaesthetic learner – you learn best by having a go at something yourself to try to understand it or watching someone else doing it.

Assessment task 3

3.1

Copy and complete Table 15.3 below. You need to identify your own learning style(s) and describe ways that you can use this information to successfully complete your childcare course.

Task	Learning style(s)	Good ways to complete the task
Finding information to make a poster about child development		
Revising for a test		
Preparing to give a presentation to the rest of your group		
Planning a craft activity for children		
Finding information to help you decide what you want to do after your college course		

Table 15.3 Identifying your learning styles and ways to successfully complete tasks

CACHE Level 1 Caring for Children

LO4 Set personal goals and objectives

It is important that you have a plan for how you will attain the skills and qualifications you need to do your chosen job role.

4.1, 4.2 Identify personal goals and describe their relevance

There are many ways to identify and set your own personal goals, for example, looking at the different job roles in your chosen career and finding out about the qualifications and skills you will need to do the job well.

Finding out about the qualifications needed for the job. **This is important when thinking about your own career progressing, e.g. wanting a job with more responsibility.**

Finding out about jobs in your chosen career. **It is important that you know about jobs that you could do now and in the future.**

Ways to set personal career goals

Improve your own skills and knowledge needed for the job. **This is important because you will need to keep up to date with changes to your job role.**

Understand the need to improve some of your qualities to do the job well. **It is important that you know when you need to improve on a quality, for example to be more patient with children.**

Figure 15.2 Ways to set personal career goals

Assessment task 4

Draw a spider diagram like the one in Figure 15.2 to identify three personal goals and describe why each of the goals are important for your own development in your chosen career.

5.1 Produce an action plan with SMART goals and actions to be taken

When you have identified your **personal goals**, you then need to think about how you can best achieve these goals. For example, once you have found out about the qualifications needed to do a job role, you might start researching local college courses next.

> ## Important words
>
> **Personal goals** – these are targets we want to achieve, such as getting a job or passing an exam.
>
> **Action plan** – a plan we can make and use to help us reach our goals.

It is important to make a written **action plan** to list your goals. Goals need to be SMART so that you identify what your goal is and understand 'how' and 'when' you will achieve it.

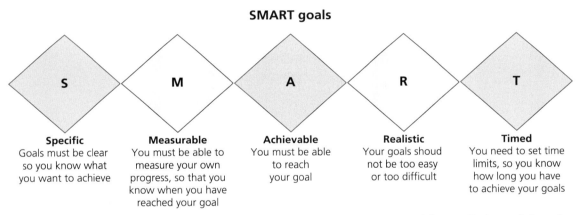

SMART goals

Specific	**Measurable**	**Achievable**	**Realistic**	**Timed**
Goals must be clear so you know what you want to achieve	You must be able to measure your own progress, so that you know when you have reached your goal	You must be able to reach your goal	Your goals shoud not be too easy or too difficult	You need to set time limits, so you know how long you have to achieve your goals

Figure 15.3 Goals should be SMART: Specific, measurable, achievable, realistic and timed

My goal is to learn to drive a car so that I can drive myself to work.	
Specific	I need to learn to drive to a safe standard.
Measurable	To pass the theory test and road test.
Achievable	I am 17 years old and I can afford to pay for the driving lessons.
Realistic	I have downloaded the theory app, I have time to learn and I have booked enough driving lessons.
Timed	I aim to pass my theory test within 6 months, and I hope to pass my driving test before I am 18 years old (in 11 months' time).

Table 15.4 An example of a SMART action plan

Action planning takes time; this can be a short or long time depending on your goal. It is important when you have a long-term goal, such as learning to drive a car, that you understand how long this might take. For example, you can have a long-term goal (ten months) to pass your test, but a good short-term goal (two weeks) may be to find an app to practise your driving theory knowledge. A medium-term goal (two months) may be to find a driving instructor and book a course of driving lessons.

Assessment task 5   (5.1)

Produce an action plan which identifies and records your personal goals which are SMART. Use Table 15.4 to help you.

Summary

In this unit you have learnt that:

◆ we use information about ourselves to choose our education and job role
◆ all our personal achievements and interests support our own development
◆ we all have things in our lives that we are good at – these are our strengths
◆ we all have areas to improve on and we can use SMART goals to do this
◆ we all have different skills, qualities and abilities and knowing what these are can help us to choose a career
◆ there are four main learning styles: visual, auditory, read and write, and kinaesthetic
◆ writing a SMART action plan can help you to reach your goals.

What you will learn in this unit

You will gain an understanding of:
- the importance of leading a healthy lifestyle
- how to get involved in doing different activities to keep you healthy
- how well different activities can help to support your healthy lifestyle.

LO1 Understand the importance of leading a healthy lifestyle

1.1, 1.2 What is a healthy lifestyle?

A **healthy lifestyle** is a way of living that lowers our risk of becoming very ill or dying early. We cannot stop ourselves from getting certain diseases, but there are some types of illnesses, such as heart disease or lung cancer, that may be avoided by having a healthy lifestyle. Scientists have found that we can cut our risk of becoming ill and can live longer by not smoking or drinking too much alcohol and by taking regular exercise, having a healthy diet, and getting sensible amounts of rest and sleep.

Health is not just about illness and disease. It is also about physical, mental and social wellbeing.

Important words

Healthy lifestyle – choosing a healthy way of life.

When adults have a healthy lifestyle, they can be seen as positive role models for children. This means that the children will see good lifestyle habits; children copy what they see, so if people working with children have healthy lifestyles, then the children will pick up these healthy habits too.

Sometimes we do not think about whether we have a healthy lifestyle, and we may not exercise enough or eat healthy foods. If we take time to think about the way we live, we can become healthier.

Figure 16.1 Living healthily makes us feel good about ourselves

Assessment task 1

Table 16.1 on the next page (page 138) gives an example of a daily diary (**personal log**). Keep a daily diary like this for three days. Write down the exercise you do, the food you eat, how much rest and sleep you get, and the social activities you take part in.

Important words

Personal log – a diary that is used to keep a record of your own lifestyle, for example, the food you ate or the exercise you did during a certain day.

Exercise	Food	Rest and sleep	Social activity
Today I played with my niece in the garden, running and kicking a ball (20 minutes). I walked to the bus stop to go to college. I tried to walk quickly so I was 'huffing and puffing' (ten minutes). I walked to my gran's house with my niece after college (five minutes each way). In the evening I played on the dance mat with my friends (one hour).	◆ Cornflakes, toast, milk and a glass of fresh orange juice (good food) ◆ Packet of crisps (not good food) ◆ Vegetable samosa, an apple and water (good food) ◆ Dried fruit snack ◆ Chicken pasta bake with cheese, peas and sweetcorn ◆ Yoghurt with berries, water ◆ I drank water throughout the day.	Woke up at 7.30 am (I went to bed at 10.30 pm so I had about nine hours' sleep.) I sat quietly with my friends during the lunch break. We sat on the grass field and looked at magazines (rested for 35 minutes). 	I spent the day with my friends at college. I played with my niece, who is four years old. I went to see my gran. I enjoy talking to her. I did my college homework for an hour and then danced on the dance mat with my friends.

Table 16.1 A personal log

The importance of exercise and activity

◆ Doing physical activity every day, such as swimming, dancing or other sports, is important for the healthy growth, development and wellbeing of children and young people.

◆ You should try to have at least 60 minutes of physical activity every day, including the kinds of activities that make you slightly out of breath, for example, walking fast or bouncing on a trampoline.

◆ You should show children that exercise and outdoor activities are enjoyable, so that they will learn that exercise is fun and a good thing to do.

◆ 'Still' time is time spent watching television, surfing the internet, chatting to friends on the phone or playing computer games. You should not spend too much time during the day doing these activities because sitting around too much and not being active enough are linked to children and adults becoming overweight or obese.

◆ If we are overweight, then this is probably because we are eating too much food for our needs and not doing enough exercise. In this situation, people should try to be more active and cut out unhealthy foods, such as fried foods, salty foods and sugary foods.

Figure 16.2 Physical activity can be enjoyable

LO2 Contribute to own health

2.1 How can we lead a healthy lifestyle?

It is often possible to make changes and do things differently to help **improve** our health and wellbeing.

Changes to lifestyle could include:
◆ doing more exercise: activities that keep us fit and healthy can be done alone (such as going for a jog in the morning) or can be done with a friend (such as playing badminton). We can also get involved in fitness activities as part of a group. These activities could involve playing football in a local team or joining a 'keep fit' or yoga class at the local sports centre
◆ stopping smoking
◆ only drinking safe amounts of alcohol
◆ not taking illegal drugs
◆ eating a healthy, balanced diet as much as possible
◆ getting enough sleep at night, especially if we need to study or work the next day.

Important words

Improve – to make better.

Assessment task 2

Look back at your daily diary (personal log) and think about three things you could change that would make you healthier. For example, you may not currently do enough exercise, or you may eat a lot of sugary foods. When you have chosen three things to try to change, put them into a table like Table 16.2. The longer you stick to any positive changes you make, the more positive effects you should see.

Activities to improve my lifestyle	Witness testimony (short description of improvement made and signature)
Example: *I spend too much time on the internet, so I will try to limit this. I will exercise for 30 minutes more every day for five days this week.*	*I went to the park to walk my Aunt Jean's dog every evening for half an hour. I did this Monday to Friday (five days).* *Signed by Jean May 14/01/2020*
1	
2	
3	

Table 16.2 Activities for a healthier lifestyle

Important words

Witness testimony – someone else's statement to prove that you have done something.

Description – a short report.

Rest and sleep

◆ Sleep is important because it gives your body a chance to rest and allows it to prepare for the next day.
◆ Sleep also gives your brain a chance to sort things out. Scientists think that sleep may be the time when the brain sorts and stores information, replaces chemicals and solves problems.
◆ The amount of sleep we need depends largely on our age. Babies sleep a lot – about 14 to 15 hours per day! But as we get older, most of us need about eight or nine hours of sleep each night.

Choose water as a drink

◆ Water is the best way to quench your thirst and **hydrate** your body (making sure that your body has enough water to work properly).
◆ Cut down on drinks with added sugar, such as soft drinks and other fizzy drinks. These are not as good at hydrating your body and can cause tooth decay.
◆ Skimmed or semi-skimmed milk is healthy to drink as it contains a lot of nutrients. It is a great source of calcium, which we need to keep our bones strong.
◆ Eat whole fruit rather than drinking fruit juices, which can have a lot of sugar in them.

A healthy diet

Figure 16.4 on the next page (page 142) shows the Eatwell Guide. It has five main food groups:
1 fruit and vegetables
2 potatoes, bread, rice, pasta and other starchy carbohydrate foods
3 beans, pulses, fish, eggs, meat and other proteins
4 dairy foods and alternatives
5 oils and spreads

Figure 16.3 A good night's sleep can contribute to a healthy lifestyle

Important words

Hydrate – replace lost water.

The five food groups contain foods that help to keep our bodies healthy. The Eatwell Guide encourages you to choose foods from the five important food groups every day.

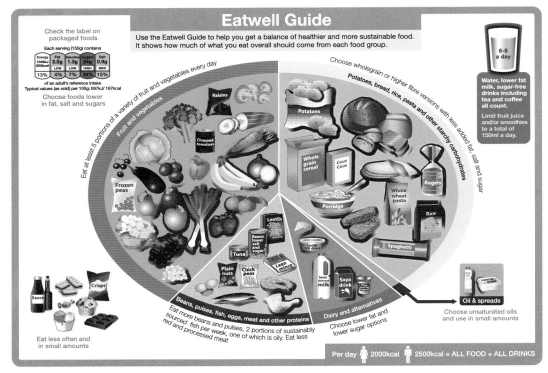

Figure 16.4 The Eatwell Guide

Eat more fruit and vegetables
◆ Eating fruit and vegetables every day helps to keep our bodies healthy.
◆ Try to eat two pieces of fruit and five servings of vegetables every day.
◆ Have fresh or dried fruit as a snack instead of sugary or salty snacks.

Personal hygiene
We should all know how to maintain good personal **hygiene**.
◆ When we look clean and smell fresh, we feel good so our self-esteem grows and we can become more confident.
◆ A smile with clean, healthy teeth can make us look and feel good.
◆ Healthy hair, skin and nails are signs of good personal hygiene and are especially important when we are around children.

Important words

Hygiene – keeping yourself clean.

- Hand washing after using the toilet or before touching food is very important. Lots of harmful germs which we cannot see live on our skin. Some germs can cause sickness, and some sickness is so serious it can make you very unwell and could even kill a baby or young child. Always wash your hands well with warm soapy water before handling any food.

- Wearing clean clothes and having a shower every day are important. If we do not keep our bodies and clothes clean, we could begin to smell. An unpleasant body smell is often caused by having unwashed bodies, so it is important to wash every day, wear clean clothes and, if necessary, wear deodorant to help you to smell fresh.

Drug awareness

Drugs can change the way our body and mind work.

- Drugs can be very addictive (the feeling that you need to take the drug more and more).
- Some drugs are illegal. It is against the law to take them, and if caught you could get into trouble with the police.
- Taking drugs can also cause mental health conditions, which can be very frightening.
- Drugs can harm our bodies and make us ill, for example, some drugs might cause **cancer**.
- Taking drugs can cost a lot of money. Some people who take drugs get into debt and may even borrow money from loan sharks or money lending companies or break the law and steal.
- Buying drugs might mean spending time with people who do not care about us and we may not be safe with them.
- Taking drugs can upset family life and cause arguments with friends, which can lead to loneliness.

There are lots of places to get help and support for problems with drugs.

Adults must never use illegal drugs when with children. Adults should be positive role models and always do their best to keep children safe.

Task

Look on the internet and find out about the support available for people worried about drugs. A good website to look at is www.talktofrank.com.

Alcohol awareness

Most people who drink alcohol consume it in safe amounts. However, some people drink too much alcohol. Drinking lots of alcohol at one time is called 'binge drinking'.

- ◆ 'Binge drinking' can cause people to become unaware of what they are doing, or even collapse and choke on their own vomit.
- ◆ When someone is not in control of their behaviour due to drinking too much, they are more likely to have unprotected sex, which can result in unwanted pregnancy or STDs/STIs (sexually transmitted diseases/infections).
- ◆ Drinking too much alcohol can cause serious damage to our bodies, such as liver disease, cancer, high blood pressure or heart attacks.
- ◆ Drinking can cause changes in behaviour. People sometimes do things that they would not usually do or go to places that could put them in great danger.
- ◆ Some people who are drunk can become very violent towards partners, family or friends.
- ◆ Pregnant women who drink can seriously harm their unborn baby, as the alcohol affects the baby growing inside them.
- ◆ Parents who drink may not be able to cope with their children or care for them properly.
- ◆ People who drink too much can feel very ill afterwards, so they might not go to college or work. This could affect their future career.

There are lots of places to get help and support for problems with drinking too much alcohol.

Adults must never use alcohol when with children. Adults should be positive role models and always do their best to keep children safe.

Task

Look on the internet and find out about the support available for people worried about alcohol. A good website to look at is www.nhs.uk/live-well/alcohol-support/.

Stop smoking

Smoking can seriously damage our health and the health of people around us. This is why it is important not to smoke or, if you have started, to try to stop.

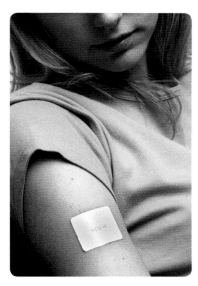

Giving up smoking helps our health to improve in many ways:
- It will reduce the risk of getting heart or lung disease.
- You will protect the health of people around you, especially children who breathe in your 'second-hand' smoke. Children sometimes develop asthma or glue ear from being around cigarette smoke.
- You will help your chances of getting pregnant in the future.
- You will improve your breathing and fitness.
- You will enjoy the taste of food more.
- You will save money.
- The health of your skin and teeth will get better.
- You and your home will smell much fresher.

If you smoke and would like to give up, then your doctor or local health centre can explain about the support available to you.

Figure 16.5 A nicotine patch: stopping smoking brings health benefits

Adults should never smoke when working with or around children and should be positive role models. Cigarette smoke in the air damages children's young lungs.

Sexual health

It is important to be aware of our sexual health and to make sure that we take good care of ourselves. We should be able to:

◆ respect ourselves and the choices which we make
◆ understand that it is important to say 'no' if we are not ready to have a sexual relationship
◆ look after our own bodies and our emotional wellbeing
◆ avoid catching sexually transmitted diseases – harmful infections that can be passed from one person to another during unprotected sex
◆ avoid unwanted pregnancies.

The more facts you know about sex and relationships, the more confident you will feel. There is a lot of information and advice available, especially on the internet. Two very good websites are www.nhs.uk/worthtalkingabout and www.nhs.uk/livewell.

Other clinics and health professionals who can offer useful information about sex, safer sex, contraception, pregnancy and sexually transmitted diseases/infections (STDs/STIs) are:

◆ a GP or nurse
◆ a midwife or health visitor
◆ a community contraceptive clinic
◆ a sexual health clinic
◆ a chemist or pharmacist.

People aged under 25 can also go to a young person's service, such as a Brook Advisory Centre.

LO3 Review the activities undertaken to maintain a healthy lifestyle

Assessment task 3

Copy and complete the personal log in Table 16.3 to **review** each of the activities you have tried to make improvements to your lifestyle.

Activity	What went well/how improvements were made	How the activity could be improved	Two more activities to support a healthy lifestyle

Table 16.3 Reviewing your activities

Important words

Review – look back and see how well something has worked.

Summary

In this unit you have learnt that:

◆ a healthy lifestyle is a way of living that keeps us fit and well

◆ a healthy lifestyle includes exercise, good food and enough sleep and rest

◆ drinking too much alcohol, taking drugs and smoking can cause serious illness or death

◆ children need to see adults with healthy lifestyles, as this will help them to learn how to stay fit and healthy themselves.

What you will learn in this unit
You will gain an understanding of:
◆ the importance of a balanced diet
◆ how families can eat well
◆ special food requirements for some people
◆ how to handle and store food safely.

LO1 The importance of a balanced diet

1.1 The main food groups

To help our bodies to grow and stay healthy, we need to eat a range of healthy foods. This is called a 'balanced diet', and to have a balanced diet, we should eat foods from the five **main food groups** every day.

These groups are:
1 fruit and vegetables
2 potatoes, bread, rice, pasta and other starchy carbohydrate foods
3 beans, pulses, fish, eggs, meat and other proteins
4 dairy foods and alternatives
5 oils and spreads

Important words

Main food groups – these are listed above; foods which are similar can be grouped together.

Foods in each of the groups have different benefits for the body:

◆ **Carbohydrates** give us energy.
◆ **Proteins** help with growth and repair.
◆ **Fats** help the body to use the vitamins and minerals found in foods.
◆ **Vitamins and minerals** help every part of the body to grow and develop healthily, such as healthy bones, strong teeth, clear skin, a healthy heart.

The Eatwell Guide on page 142 shows the food groups which appear in a balanced diet.

1.2 What is a balanced diet?

Table 17.1 shows all the main **nutrients** that make up a balanced diet. It shows examples of foods which the nutrients can be found in and the benefits for the body.

> **Important words**
>
> **Nutrients** – these are contained within foods and do very important jobs in the body to keep people healthy.

Nutrient	Foods it is found in	Benefits for the body
Carbohydrate	Bread, pasta, couscous, flour, potatoes and bananas	Gives the body energy.
Protein	Meat, eggs, fish, milk and other dairy products For vegetarians/vegans: wheat, oats, pulses, lentils, tofu and soya products (e.g. veggie burgers)	Helps the body to repair cells. Helps the body to grow and develop well.
Fats	Butter, margarine, vegetable oil, fish and dairy products	Gives the body energy. Helps the body to be able to use vitamins A and D.
Vitamin A	Carrots, milk, apricots, oily fish and margarine	Good for healthy eyes and clear eyesight.
Vitamin B	Bread, meat, yeast, pasta, flour, rice and noodles	Good for a healthy nervous system. Helps the body to release energy from other foods.

Table 17.1 The main nutrients of a balanced diet

Nutrient	Foods it is found in	Benefits for the body
Vitamin C	Oranges, lemons, sweet potatoes, grapefruits, blackcurrants, kiwis and potatoes	Good for healthy gums and skin.
Vitamin E	Vegetable oil, green leafy vegetables (e.g. spinach), nuts and wheatgerm	Works as an **antioxidant**, protecting the eyes, liver and skin tissues from environmental pollution.
Vitamin K	Most fresh vegetables, yoghurt, lean meat and eggs	Helps the blood to clot: after an injury it helps the bleeding to slow down and eventually stop. Keeps bones strong and healthy.
Iron	Red meat, broccoli, spinach, pak choi, egg yolk, plain chocolate and dried fruits	Helps the blood to carry oxygen through the body. During pregnancy, the mother's iron helps the baby's brain to develop and work properly.
Calcium	Milk, cheese, butter, yoghurt and other dairy products, cereals and grains	Good for healthy bones and teeth. Also helps to keep our hearts healthy.

Table 17.1 The main nutrients of a balanced diet *(Continued)*

Important words

Antioxidant – these work to reverse the effects of pollution on the body.

Task

Write down everything you ate yesterday. Do you think you ate a balanced diet? Look at the different food groups. Did you eat the right amounts of nutrients to give you a balanced diet?

1.3 The effect of diet on health

At different times in our lives, our bodies have different nutritional needs. The foods which we eat sometimes need to change to give us the correct balanced diet.

> **Example!**
>
> Most children and teenagers grow quickly, so they need to have more protein and carbohydrates. Breastfeeding mothers should have slightly more fats in their diet as this helps them to produce milk for the baby.

Assessment task 1

1 On the back of a paper plate, write down the meaning of a balanced diet.
2 Divide the plate into the five main food groups and list a few foods that would go into each group.
3 List five ways in which eating a balanced diet can keep a person healthy.

LO2 Good eating habits for families

2.1 The importance of family mealtimes

Families and households can lead very busy lives and sometimes do not spend much time together. This can make some members of a family feel that they are not talking to each other enough. If it is possible for the family to sit and eat together, mealtimes can give them the chance to talk to each other.

Figure 17.1 Family mealtimes are important

Task

Think about mealtimes in your home:
◆ Do you eat meals with your family or the other people in your home?
◆ Do you have good eating habits?
◆ Write down what you can do to set a good example for a child at a dinner table.

Mealtimes spent together as a family also help family members to:
◆ share thoughts and feelings or worries they may have (for example, how you are doing at college)
◆ talk about the food they eat (for example, talking about healthy food will teach children about how to stay healthy)
◆ teach younger children table manners (for example, sitting up at the table and using utensils, such as serving spoons, knives, forks or chopsticks)
◆ tempt children to try foods they have not eaten before (for example, a child who eats a lot of sweet foods might be tempted to try vegetables if they see an older brother or sister eating them).

Assessment task 2

1 Draw a spider diagram to show four reasons why it is important for families to eat together regularly.
2 Draw another spider diagram to show ways that adults can encourage children to eat healthy foods.
3 Draw or write down one example of a healthy meal that could be given to a child (think about including foods from the five food groups).

Regular meals which families eat together can be an important and comforting part of a child's daily routine. It is not only dinner that can be eaten together, but also breakfast. Breakfast is a very important meal that gives us the energy we need to start the day. Cars need fuel to get from one place to another; our bodies are the same and our fuel is food.

2.2 How to encourage children to eat healthily

There are many ways to encourage children to eat well and choose healthy foods:

◆ Make healthy choices interesting. Many recipe books show simple, healthy meals and snacks which look inviting and attractive for children to eat.

◆ You can cut food into interesting shapes or make a face using the ingredients. Also try giving food special names, such as 'cool carrots' and 'brilliant broccoli'.

◆ Allow children to get involved. Helping with the shopping can teach children about how to recognise healthy products. Older children can look at the food labels and even see which nutrients the food contains.

◆ Home-cooked meals usually provide healthy options. Children can watch food being prepared and cooked using healthy ingredients, and can help out with making healthy meals. 'Fast food' usually contains more fat, sugar and salt than home cooking.

◆ Children like to copy people around them, so adults should always try to be positive role models. Eat healthily in front of children so that they can see how important it is. Also, talk about healthy food using positive language.

◆ Make healthy snacks for hungry moments – bowls of fresh and dried fruits, or chopped, raw vegetables with vegetable dips and olives.

◆ Try not to give children too many snacks between meals or let them fill up on fizzy drinks. This will spoil their appetite for healthy meals.

Figure 17.2 Healthy snacks can be fun!

Avoid using food as a reward for good behaviour or as a bribe to get a child to do something. This may cause them to develop unhealthy eating habits.

Healthy meals for children

It is important to spend time thinking about how to make healthy meals for children. Adults can then be sure that the children are getting a good, balanced diet. Children's diets should also have enough energy (measured in calories) to help them grow and develop healthily.

Some things that need to be included in healthy meals include:

◆ up to five servings of fruit and vegetables every day
◆ foods that contain iron, such as meat and fish, or rice and lentils for children who do not eat meat
◆ foods that contain calcium, such as dairy products
◆ starchy food – potatoes, pasta and brown bread – are a better way of getting energy than sugary foods
◆ a drink: whole cow's milk for children from 12 months old; diluted fresh fruit juice with a meal is a good way of getting vitamin C.

Children should drink plenty of water throughout the day to prevent them from being thirsty. If they are thirsty, they are already dehydrated (need water).

Task

Which of these meals do you think has the most nutrients in it and why?
◆ Sausage and mashed potatoes, water to drink
◆ Tuna sandwiches, green peppers, cheese and milk
◆ Spaghetti with cheese and butter, and a fizzy drink
◆ Egg and chips, water to drink
◆ Fish fingers, spaghetti and a fizzy drink

LO3 Special food requirements for different groups

There are people who cannot eat certain foods because of health or religious reasons. Adults working with young children need to understand the different diets, religious beliefs, cultures and lifestyles of families so that they can support their wishes, special diets, customs and eating habits.

3.1 Food restrictions for religious groups

People from different cultures or religious groups may have particular foods that they prefer to eat. The food that they eat will often be different because of their individual needs and beliefs.

Important words

Food restrictions – when a certain type of food should not be handled or eaten for health or religious reasons.

Example!

Examples of religious groups are:
1 Hindus (Hinduism)
2 Rastafarians (Rastafarianism)
3 Jews (Judaism)
4 Muslims (Islam)
5 Buddhists (Buddhism)
6 Christians (Christianity).

Hindus

People who practise the Hindu religion do not usually eat beef (meat from a cow). This is because Hindus believe that the cow is a sacred or holy animal that should never be eaten. Strict Hindus will not eat meat or even eggs, as they are also seen as having life. Fat, such as lard, is not eaten, as it is an animal fat.

Figure 17.3 Hindus do not eat beef and many do not eat meat at all

Figure 17.4 Celebrating different religious festivals can be fun for young children and can support their knowledge of different cultures

Rastafarians

People who follow the Rastafarian religion believe that it is very important to live a pure life and eat simple foods. This means that they may prefer to live close to nature and grow fresh food on the land. Rastafarians like to keep their bodies pure and healthy, so may choose not to drink alcohol, tea and coffee. There are also rules about the fish and meat they can eat, so many Rastafarians choose to follow a vegan diet.

Muslims

People who follow the Muslim religion (Islam) will usually only prepare and eat food which is **halal**. This means that the animal has been slaughtered in a way which is approved by Islam. Muslims do not eat pork, or drink alcohol. Adults will usually **fast** (not eat food) during the holy month of Ramadan.

Jews

Many people who practise the Jewish religion follow certain rules about food. One rule is to only prepare and eat food that is **kosher** (prepared according to Jewish law). Like Muslims, Jews do not eat pork.

Buddhists

Most Buddhists choose to be vegetarians (to not eat meat) so that they can avoid harming or killing any animals. Some Buddhists do not eat fish for the same reason.

Christians

There are no particular dietary requirements for many Christian groups, but some Christians **fast** (do not eat certain foods) at special times of year. Some foods are important for religious festivals, such as Easter and Shrove Tuesday, also known as Pancake Day.

Assessment task 4a

Make a poster that gives information on the foods that should not be eaten by people from four religious groups.

3.2 Special dietary requirements

As well as understanding about foods which people do or do not eat for religious reasons, we also need to be aware of the **special diets** that some people follow because of health reasons and lifestyle choices.

Some individuals or families may choose not to eat any meat or fish. They may choose to follow a vegetarian or a vegan diet.

Important words

Special diet – when a person has a food restriction, so can only eat the foods which they are allowed.

Vegetarian diet

Vegetarians do not eat meat or fish. They usually prefer to eat food that comes from plants, such as fruit and vegetables. Vegetarians often eat grains, nuts and seeds with vegetables. These may include rice, lentils or pasta. Vegetarians may eat dairy produce, such as cheese and yoghurt and also eggs. People who do not eat meat but do eat fish are called pescatarians.

Vegan diet

People following a vegan diet do not eat meat, fish, eggs or any dairy produce. Many vegans choose not to eat anything that has been made using any part of the animal. This may include animal fats, wine, sauces and even honey because it is made by bees.

Vegans do not wear leather or fur, as both of these products are made from animals.

3.3 Food allergies

Having a **food allergy** means that eating or sometimes touching a certain food can cause a person to become ill.

Important words

Food allergy – when a person cannot have a certain food because they will become ill after eating or touching it.

Important words

Allergic reaction – when somebody eats or touches food that they are allergic to and their body is affected.

Anaphylactic shock – a life threatening allergic reaction.

Assessment task 4b

1   Write down what vegetarians do and do not eat in their diet.
2   Cut out pictures of three foods that can cause some people to have an allergic reaction.

If a person has an allergy to a certain food, they should avoid eating it. An **allergic reaction** can happen when somebody eats the food which they are allergic to and they become ill. The reaction could be relatively minor, for example, a headache, runny nose or itchy eyes, or it could be much more severe, such as going into **anaphylactic shock**. Some babies and children have food allergies that are so severe that if a certain food is eaten it could cause death. It is VERY IMPORTANT that you are aware of any food allergies that a child has and you MUST make sure that the child does not come into contact with these foods.

The most common foods that children are allergic to are:
◆   milk
◆   peanuts and tree nuts
◆   eggs
◆   wheat
◆   fish (including shellfish: mussels, prawns and crab).

LO4 How to handle and store food safely

Important words

Food handling – buying, storing and preparing food correctly, so that it is safe to eat.

4.1 Personal hygiene, handling and storing food safely

It is very important to have good personal hygiene when you are preparing or handling food.

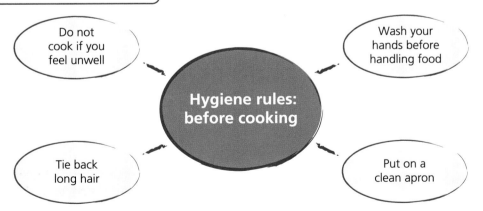

Figure 17.5a Excellent hygiene is essential in the workplace (examples of hygiene rules to follow before cooking)

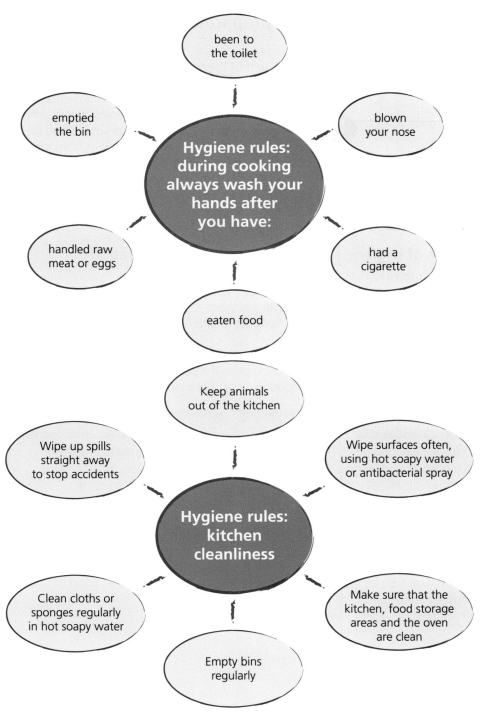

Figure 17.5b and c Excellent hygiene is essential in the workplace (hygiene rules during cooking/handwashing, and kitchen cleanliness)

4.2, 4.3 Food storage and preparation to stop cross contamination

It is very important to store food safely, so that the food is good to eat and free from germs and bacteria. One hazard of poor food storage is **cross contamination**. Some foods are not safe to eat raw because they have germs on them which are removed only during cooking, which then makes the food safe to eat. Cross contamination happens when the germs from raw foods, in this instance, are passed on to cooked foods, which are then eaten. This can make you very ill. Cross contamination can also mean when food which some people are allergic to touches other food and could cause an allergic reaction.

Important words

Cross contamination – germs or bacteria from one type of food spread to another food, or food that people are allergic spreads to another food.

Examples of hygiene rules: to avoid cross contamination

- Defrost frozen food before cooking, if required.
- Make sure that food is cooked all the way through, especially meat and fish.
- Keep hot food hot and cold food cold.
- Keep separate knives, dishes and chopping boards for raw and cooked foods to stop cross contamination.
- Wrap or cover food and put it away in the fridge or cupboard as soon as it is cool.
- Make sure that raw meat and fish are kept at the bottom of the fridge to stop them dripping onto cooked food and causing cross contamination.

Assessment task 5

You have been asked to help prepare food for a child's party. You will be making egg sandwiches, falafels, hummus, sushi, cheese chunks, tomatoes, cucumber slices, jelly and ice cream. There will be fruit juice to drink.

1. Write down three reasons why you should wash your hands before starting to prepare the food.
2. Write down one food storage rule you should follow to keep the food safe to eat.
3. Write down one way in which this food can be prepared safely.
4. Write down three ways in which you can stop cross contamination of raw and cooked foods.

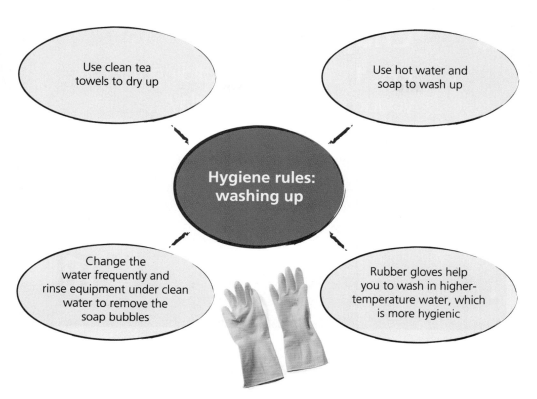

Figure 17.6 Hygiene rules for washing up

> ## Summary
> In this unit you have learnt that:
> - a balanced diet is important for a person's health
> - it is important for children that families have good eating habits
> - some people have different food requirements and need special diets
> - it is important to handle and store food safely to stop cross contamination from causing illness.

Chapter 18
CFC 1 Confidence building for the young child through play

What you will learn in this unit

You will gain an understanding of:

◆ activities that help a child to express their feelings
◆ activities that help to build a child's confidence
◆ the support a young child might need to gain confidence through play
◆ the encouragement a young child might need to express their feelings through play.

LO1 Support a child to gain confidence through play

1.1 Play activities to build a child's confidence

Activities for children can help to **build** their confidence. However, it is very important to make sure that the child has the right support from the adult, and that the activity is at the right level for the child's age and ability. A suitable activity is one that is neither too easy nor too difficult. For example, if the child is too young to hold a pencil and control the marks they make on the page, asking them to copy their name might damage their confidence and they may not want to try to use a pencil again.

Figure 18.1 Children's confidence can be boosted by completing an activity successfully

Important words

Build confidence – like a wall being built, confidence can be built up with the support of an adult.

Express feelings – show others how you are feeling.

Attempting this activity could damage the child's confidence because they may feel that they are 'not good enough' or 'not clever', when actually they are just too young for this type of activity.

It is very important that when the adult plans an activity, they understand what each child enjoys doing. By including a child's interests in the planning, adults can give the child the chance to learn, at the same time as having fun doing something that they enjoy. Adults need to give the child the opportunity to learn new things and develop new skills, but they must make sure that the child can complete the activity successfully, as this will help to build the child's confidence.

1.2 Supporting children to gain confidence in an activity

Supporting a child to **gain confidence** is a very important part of childcare. Adults can easily damage a child's confidence, and it is sometimes very difficult for a child to rebuild it.

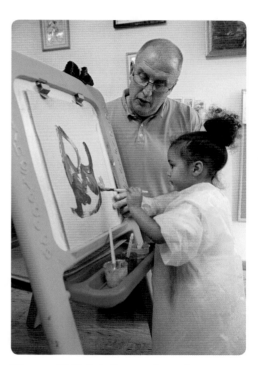

There are many ways that an adult can support children to gain confidence during play. It is essential that adults think about how to help children become confident. The following could be helpful:

◆ providing appropriate activities for the child
◆ providing suitable equipment for the child, such as suitable scissors (remember some left-handed pairs)
◆ giving the child praise and encouragement
◆ helping the child to do the activity if they are finding it difficult
◆ enabling the child to do it themselves if they can.

Children need to understand that it is alright to make mistakes, as this is part of how they learn. Their confidence can be easily damaged if they try something and are not good at it. They may feel embarrassed about trying again, so adults need to praise the child for trying and encourage them to have another go.

Figure 18.2 Adults can boost children's confidence by praising their efforts

Important words

Gain confidence – when children develop more belief in themselves and what they are able to do.

Assessment task 1

Sana is four and a half years old. List three activities that would be suitable to help build Sana's confidence. Write down how the adult could support Sana during the activities to help build her confidence.

LO2 Encourage children to show their feelings through play

Important words

Self-esteem – how much you value or how much worth you place on yourself.

2.1 Activities which support children to show their feelings

Some activities give adults the opportunity to support children's **self-esteem**. Examples are shown in Table 18.1.

Activity	The adult's role in supporting the child's self-esteem
Circle time	Adults should give every child the chance to talk about themselves and be listened to. This supports the child to feel valued and helps build their self-esteem.
Stories and books	Stories sometimes make children think about different feelings, so adults should take time to listen and comfort the child if they feel frightened, sad or angry. Adults should also share in children's feelings of happiness and encourage this. This helps to build a child's self-esteem.
A trip to the shops	A trip like this can enable children to gain confidence in their ability to keep themselves safe, e.g. if children learn how to cross a road safely or walk sensibly along a path, they will be praised by the adults for learning about road safety. This will make them feel they are responsible and will build their self-esteem.
Giving children responsibilities	When children are given little tasks or responsibilities (such as pouring the juice or feeding the nursery rabbit), they feel proud of themselves and this builds their self-esteem.
Painting and drawing	When children create pictures, they sometimes show their feelings. Children do not always think about what they are painting; they may just want to enjoy feeling the paint move on the paper or watch the colours mix. Adults should say, 'Tell me about the picture' rather than ask 'What have you painted?'; this enables children to talk about feelings if they want to. The child will feel that the adult is interested and this will support their self-esteem.

Table 18.1 Activities which can boost children's self-esteem

2.2 Supporting a child's self-esteem

Self-esteem is how you feel about yourself. Good self-esteem means that you have positive thoughts about yourself, for example, 'I will have a go and if I make a mistake that's ok, I will try again.'

Our self-esteem suffers when we do not feel good about ourselves, for example, feeling 'I am not good at anything' or 'I always make mistakes so I am not going to have a go because I will get it wrong.'

Task

In small groups, think of something that you each found difficult at school.

Think about how you felt: were you given good support and encouragement to try again, or were you criticised and not confident enough to have another go?

Think about the support and encouragement you received from adults: did this affect how you felt about yourself?

Figure 18.3 Children have a good chance to be listened to during circle time

Ways to help children build good self-esteem include:

◆ Learning the child's name and using it correctly, so that they feel you are interested in them.
◆ Always listening carefully when the child is talking. If a child tells you they feel sad, take the time to talk to them about these feelings and try and comfort them.
◆ Showing the child that you are interested in what they are doing, for example, 'What do you most like playing with in the nursery?'
◆ Using supportive words and body language when talking and listening to the child, for example, smiling and saying 'What a lovely painting! Tell me about it.'

Assessment task 2

Write down two activities for children aged three to four years and say how the adult could support the child during the activities so that the child can develop good self-esteem.

Summary

In this unit you have learnt that:

◆ children's confidence and self-esteem can be developed by caring and supportive adults
◆ play activities are a very good way to build children's confidence
◆ some play activities give children the opportunity to talk about or act out their feelings
◆ children need to know that it is alright to make mistakes, as that is how they learn.

CACHE Level 1 Caring for Children

Group B

Chapter 19
CFC 2 Listening to and talking with a young child

What you will learn in this unit

You will gain an understanding of:

◆ the skills that adults need to use when communicating with young children

◆ activities that will help to develop children's talking and listening skills

◆ the role of the adult in supporting talking and listening activities.

LO1 Skills for communicating with a young child

1.1 How an adult can be responsive when listening to children

To listen to children properly, adults need to give them their full attention when they are speaking. Here are some tips for being a good active listener:

◆ Give your full attention to the child who is speaking. This will show them that you are listening and interested in what they have to say. This will encourage the child to talk.

◆ Do not look around the room when the child is talking to you. Make sure you look at them. Again, this will show that you are interested and value them.

◆ Make sure your mind is focused on the child and what they are saying. It is easy to let your mind wander and you may miss what the child is trying to say. This may result in the adult missing important information that the child is giving.

◆ Let the child finish speaking before you begin to talk. When you interrupt, the child may think that you are not listening, even if you are. The child may stop talking and move away.

- Use positive **body language**, such as nodding your head or looking concerned. This will let the child know that you are hearing what they are saying.
- Listen out for the main ideas and ask the child questions if you are not sure that you fully understand.

For example, you might say 'How did you get to the seaside, on the coach?' or 'Tell me again about your sore leg.' This will help you to fully understand the information that is being given.

Important words

Body language – how a person might stand, or the movements they make that show how they feel or what they may be thinking.

Figure 19.1 It is important to listen to young children

Assessment task 1

Complete the following task in pairs, with one person acting as the listener, the other as the talker:

- The talker can tell the listener about something important to them, such as what they did at the weekend, or their favourite television programme.
- The listener can use two ways to show the talker that they are interested and listening to what they are saying. An example is smiling or nodding the head.
- Write down the ways in which a person can actively listen to what somebody is saying to them.

1.2 Active listening

Active listening is very important when caring for young children. When we are talking to people, we often do not listen very well – we only think we do. Actually, we may be only half listening!

Listening properly to children will help to make them feel important and well cared for; this helps them to develop good confidence and self-esteem.

If we do not listen carefully to children, they may feel unimportant, which could damage their self-esteem. They may be trying to tell you something that is very important to them. If this is ignored, the adult may even be putting the child's life at risk, for example, the child may be trying to tell you that someone is hurting them and that they are worried.

Figure 19.2 Body language is important when working with children

As well as listening, good communication with children means that the adult needs to communicate well. Tips for communicating well with children include:

◆ Speak clearly and try to pronounce words correctly. This will help children to speak correctly.
◆ Use simple sentences with young children so that they understand what you mean, for example, 'Tidy up time'.
◆ Get down to the child's level and show positive body language, for example, stand slightly back to give the child space.
◆ Use appropriate facial expressions, for example, if the child is telling you that something is hurting, show concern through your facial expressions. You could damage a child's self-esteem if they feel that you do not care.
◆ Use **open-ended questions**. These are questions that do not encourage the child to give one-word answers, such as 'yes' or 'no'.
◆ Use appropriate language. Always use words that support the child. *Never* swear or use bad language in front of the child.
◆ Never shout at a child. You should only shout if the child is in serious danger, such as walking too close to a moving swing.

Important words

Active listening – when you listen carefully to a person who is talking, using body language to show them that you are interested.

Open-ended questions – questions that are asked in a certain way so that the answer gives more information than just 'yes' or 'no'.

Task

Read the following sentences. Which ones are open-ended questions?

(Remember, these are questions that *do not* require one-word answers.)

1 Tell me about your new coat.
2 Is your new coat warm?
3 Did you do anything interesting at the weekend?
4 What did you do at the weekend?

Write down two more open-ended questions that would be suitable to ask young children.

LO2 Activities to support children's talking and listening skills

2.1, 2.2, 2.3 List activities and identify the adult's and child's role

Activity	The role of the adult	The role of the child
Books (suitable for all ages)	◆ Choose a range of books for the age of the child. Picture books are suitable for young babies and longer stories for older children. ◆ Read the story well, using different voices for each character. ◆ Always read the story first to make sure that it is suitable and that they can read all the words. ◆ Listen to the children repeating words and encourage them by saying, 'well done'. ◆ Listen to the children retell the story and help them if they forget what happens next.	◆ Enable the child to choose a book from the selection. ◆ Younger children could repeat sounds or words from the book. ◆ Older children can listen to the story, then act it out or tell it again in their own words.

Table 19.1 Activities that will develop children's listening skills

Activity	The role of the adult	The role of the child
Circle time (suitable for children aged four and five years)	◆ Organise a few children to sit in a small circle. ◆ Explain the rules to the children, for example, 'We listen to each other and take turns to talk.' ◆ Give children the chance to talk; this could be about their favourite toy or what they did at the weekend. ◆ Listen to what each child is saying and remember the things they enjoy.	◆ Think about what they want to say and perhaps bring in a toy or object from home for 'show and tell'. ◆ Listen to each other and follow the rules of circle time by taking turns to speak.
Songs and rhymes (suitable for all children from birth)	◆ Learn suitable songs and nursery rhymes. ◆ Encourage the children to join in and learn the actions. ◆ Listen to the children when they suggest songs to sing.	◆ Listen to the song. ◆ Remember some of the words and repeat them. ◆ Try and learn some of the actions.

Table 19.1 Activities that will develop children's listening skills *(Continued)*

Activity	The role of the adult	The role of the child
A trip to the park (suitable for children aged three to five years)	◆ Plan a safe route to walk to the park and share this with other adults. ◆ Make sure there are enough adults for the number of children. ◆ Explain to the children where they are going. ◆ Tell the children about keeping safe. ◆ Listen to the children when they are telling you about what they enjoyed most.	◆ Listen carefully to instructions given by the adult. ◆ Talk about how they feel about the trip, e.g. happy, worried. ◆ Ask questions so that they understand what they will be doing. ◆ Talk about the trip when they return.

Table 19.1 Activities that will develop children's listening skills *(Continued)*

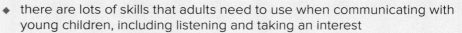

Summary

In this unit you have learnt that:

◆ there are lots of skills that adults need to use when communicating with young children, including listening and taking an interest

◆ some activities are good for developing children's talking and listening skills

◆ adults can support children to be good talkers and to understand that it is important to listen to others.

Glossary

Abilities – these are things we are able to do.

Achievement – this is something that you successfully managed to do.

Action plan – a plan we can make and use to help us reach our goals.

Active listening – when you listen carefully to a person who is talking, using body language to show them that you are interested.

Allergic reaction – when somebody eats or touches food that they are allergic to and their body is affected.

Anaphylactic shock – a life threatening allergic reaction.

An experiment – a test to see how something works or what might happen.

Antioxidant – these work to reverse the effects of pollution on the body.

Areas for further development – these are things that we need to improve or get better at.

Auditory learner – you learn best by listening to information or taking part in group discussions.

Autism – a condition that affects how a child develops, communicates and relates to other people and how they experience the world around them.

Barriers – things that may get in the way of achievement.

Body language – how a person might stand, or the movements they make that show how they feel or what they may be thinking.

Broaden children's experiences – giving children the opportunity to take part in a wide range of activities or experiences, locally and within the wider environment.

Build confidence – like a wall being built, confidence can be built up with the support of an adult.

Career – a job that you do for a long or extended period of time, and can take you in a certain direction, for example, childcare or nursing.

Career goals – what you want to achieve from your career.

Career path – the direction in which a person takes their career.

(Career) progression – being able to move on to the job you want to do, or to get promotion.

Challenge discrimination – when we take action to make sure that no child feels left out or bullied because of what they can do or how they look.

Circumstances or life events – situations or experiences in a person's life.

Cleaning products – liquids or powders used to clean floors, cookers or carpets, for example.

Contribute – add to.

Craft activity – making something with your hands.

Cross contamination – germs or bacteria from one type of food spread to another food, or food that people are allergic to spreads to another food.

Culture – the way someone lives, including the ideas, customs and behaviour they have within a society.

Curiosity – interest that is shown to learn new things or gain knowledge.

CV – a list of your skills and knowledge.

Description – a short report.

Discrimination – an instance where an individual is disadvantaged because of a protected characteristic, such as disability or religion.

Electronic toys – toys and games that need power to work, usually from electricity or batteries.

Emotional and social wellbeing – happiness in yourself and as part of a group (society).

Emotional development – the development of many different feelings, from sad to happy and excited to angry.

Emotional wellbeing – feeling happy in yourself and feeling positive.

Experiment – test or try out new things.

Express feelings – show others how you are feeling.

Facial expressions – these are the ways our faces change (or the look on our faces change), which others use to understand what we mean.

Factors affecting physical growth and development – negative or positive experiences that change how we grow or develop.

Factors preventing children from taking part in leisure activities – things that stop children from taking part.

Features of a setting – the appearance and description of a room or place.

Fire hazard – something that may cause a fire.

Food allergy – when a person cannot have a certain food because they will become ill after eating or touching it.

Food handling – buying, storing and preparing food correctly, so that it is safe to eat.

Food restrictions – when a certain type of food should not be handled or eaten for health or religious reasons.

Gain confidence – when children develop more belief in themselves and what they are able to do.

Health and safety guidelines/guidance – information about how to stay healthy and safe.

Health and safety instructions – rules that are given to follow to keep people safe.

Health and safety risks – any harm or injury that may take place; things or situations that could be dangerous and cause harm.

Health and safety symbols – signs or stamps used to show that something is safe to use.

Healthy lifestyle – choosing a healthy way of life.

Hydrate – replace lost water.

Hygiene – keeping yourself clean.

Improve – to make better.

Intellectual development – when our brain develops and we begin to understand more, for example, children learn to read and write.

Investigate – find out (about something).

Job – work that you do in order to earn money.

Kinaesthetic – you learn best by having a go at something yourself to try to understand it or watching someone else doing it.

Language development – this starts when a baby is born and begins to communicate by crying. The baby hears sounds and begins to copy what they have heard. This is the beginning of language development.

Learning style – this is the way we learn best; we may have more than one learning style.

Leisure activities – activities or hobbies that people might enjoy.

Leisure facilities – places which provide an opportunity to relax and enjoy activities.

Lifestyle – the ways in which a person lives their life and the choices which they make.

Local community – the places and people near to where we live.

Main food groups – these are listed on page 148; foods which are similar can be grouped together.

Make improvements – to get better at something.

Milestones – these are targets that children reach at certain points in their development, for example, most babies can sit up by eight months.

Musical instruments – objects that make musical sounds.

Natural environment – green spaces, which may be planted with trees, contain rivers or be used as parks.

Nutrients – these are contained within foods and do very important jobs in the body to keep people healthy.

Observe – look at or watch.

Open-ended questions – questions that are asked in a certain way so that the answer gives more information than just 'yes' or 'no'.

Own strengths – these are things that we are good at.

Pathway – a timeline.

Patterns or stages of development – when a baby or child develops a skill and can then move on to develop another more difficult skill. For example, the next stage of development for a baby who can stand will be to walk while holding onto an adult's hand.

Personal goals – these are targets we want to achieve, such as getting a job or passing an exam.

Personal log – a diary that is used to keep a record of your own lifestyle, for example, the food you ate or the exercise you did during a certain day.

Personality – how a person thinks and behaves.

Physical development – when our bodies grow and we gain new skills, for example, jumping and riding a bike.

Policies and procedures – these are the rules of the setting, which need to be followed at all times when working with babies and children.

Positive learning environment – a room or place that supports children's learning.

Potential hazard – a possible problem or danger.

Protected characteristic – a specific aspect of a person's identity defined by the Equality Act and protected by law from discrimination.

Qualities – these are good parts of our personality.

Read and write – you learn best by reading information and taking notes.

Recommended – suggested because it is important.

Recruitment – how a person with the right skills can be found and chosen for the right job.

Recruitment process – applying for a job, preparing and going for an interview. From the employer's side, this involves advertising the job vacancy, interviewing and hiring the right person.

Research – finding information, for example from the internet, books or by speaking to others.

Resilience – being able to cope with a situation or feeling.

Resources – the equipment and tools needed for an activity; toys and equipment.

Respecting children – this is when you feel and behave positively towards children.

Review – look back and see how well something has worked.

Safety equipment – equipment that keeps adults and children safe, such as car seats or fire blankets.

Safety features – a part of an object that makes it safe to use, such as seatbelts in a car.

Self-esteem – how much you value or how much worth you place on yourself.

Senses – sight, hearing, touch, smell and taste: used to make sense of the world around us.

Sensitive hearing – when someone is aware of very small sounds.

Sensory aid – objects or materials used by children to encourage the use of their senses when learning.

Skills – something we are able to do well.

Social development – understanding the needs of others as well as your own and understanding how to behave in different places.

Special diet – when a person has a food restriction, so can only eat the foods which they are allowed.

Stamina – ability to keep going for a long time, for example with exercise.

Stereotyping – believing that a group of people, or a person, have a certain characteristic, which might not be accurate.

Technology toys – toys which usually have some kind of simple built-in computer.

Training – courses which help a person to gain skills or qualifications.

Visual learner – you learn best by looking at diagrams and symbols.

Wellbeing – health.

Witness testimony – someone else's statement to prove that you have done something.

Index